The Tao of the Vow:

The Path to *YOUR* Perfect Vows

Also by J. Thomas Steele

Questions for Couples: What to Ask Before You Say “I Do”: A Primer for Planning Your Future Together and A Guide to What to Expect From Premarital Counseling

YOUR Wedding Speech Made Easy: The "How-to" Guide for The Couple (Writing and Delivering YOUR Perfect Wedding Speech)

YOUR Wedding Speech Made Easy: The “How-to” Guide for the Father of the Bride, the Best Man . . . and Everyone Else! (Writing and Delivering YOUR Perfect Wedding Speech)

The Tao of the Vow:

The Path to *YOUR* Perfect Vows

How to Write and Deliver *Your* Wedding Vows

Book 2 in *The Wedding Series*

J. Thomas Steele

Disclaimer:
The author assumes no responsibility nor is liable for adverse effects resulting from the use of advice or information contained in this book. This book is sold with the understanding that the information provided is for informational purposes only and does not offer or provide any legal or professional advice. This book does not contain all information available on the subject. This book should be considered a general guide and not as the ultimate source of information. The author and publisher shall have no liability or responsibility to any person or entity regarding any loss or damaged incurred, directly or indirectly, by the information contained in this book.

ISBN 13-978-1535254823

ISBN 10-1535254823

First Edition

10 9 8 7 6 5 4 3 2 1

Dedication

To my late parents who showed me how a marriage should work. To my wonderful wife who shows me every day. To my son and soon-to-be daughter-in-law who inspired this effort And to my daughter who may have a use for this book—though not too soon, I hope.

But mostly to all of you who are about to be wed:

Good Luck, Good Health, Long Life and Love Always!

"Knowledge is of two kinds. We know a subject ourselves, or we know where we can find information upon it."

--Samuel Johnson (1709-1784) English writer, poet, essayist, and lexicographer

Dear Reader,

Thank you for choosing my book to "find information upon it." I hope that you find everything you are looking for. I wrote this book to be informative, helpful and entertaining, and trust you will find it so.

Happy Reading!

J. Thomas Steele

Table of Contents

A Note About the Book Cover

The book cover is from the ink and color on silk painting, *Bamboo and Cranes,* by Bian Jingzhao, a famed Chinese painter from the early Ming Dynasty. His paintings were so highly skilled that he received an appointment from the Emperor Chengzu who ruled from 1403 to 1424.

I thought this painting was appropriate for this book because:

+ The Emperor titled his reign the "Yongle" period, which means "Time of Perpetual Happiness." And isn't that what we seek when we marry?

+ Bamboo is a fast growing, evergreen grass symbolizing long life and vitality. And isn't that also what we seek when we marry?

+ Lastly, cranes mate for life and have always been a symbol of long lasting togetherness. And isn't that . . .

"Bamboo and Cranes" from "The Time of Perpetual Happiness." A symbolic portrait of what I hope you, dear reader, will indeed find.

. . .

The back cover is a detail from the 12th Century Autumn landscape painting on silk attributed to the Chinese Emperor Huizong of Song.

Both paintings are in the public domain.

Introduction

If you are looking for a quick, 5-minute way to write your vows, this is ***NOT*** the book for you.

This book will require both work and your commitment. Why? Because nothing worthwhile is ever easy.

And, what could be more worthwhile than stating your love and intentions to the person with whom you wish to spend the rest of your life? What could be better than personalizing this particularly precious moment, endowing it with even *more* meaning?

If you want to learn how to write a vow from the depths of your heart, to express in words the truest love and deepest commitment you feel, and if you want to learn techniques that can help you write and deliver speeches well beyond your vows—techniques you can adapt for school or business—then this book ***IS*** for you!

Be prepared to learn. Be prepared to work. As with anything you do, you will only get out of this what you put into it. I don't mean to scare you off, or discourage you. I simply want you to understand what it is you must do to write your perfect vows.

But don't worry—you *will* learn and the work *will* be easier than you think, indeed, it may turn out to be a pleasure! Follow The Path, follow the guidelines, use the information in the appendices, and you *will* learn how to write and deliver your vows, a little about yourself, and methods you can apply to other aspects of your life.

It is my hope that by following the suggestions in this book you will write vows that will show a balance between the traditional, the trendy, your hopes and expectations, and your individuality (uniqueness). For over forty years, I have helped couples write both their vows and wedding speeches, and I sincerely thank you for allowing me to play some small part in your special day.

Note: Obviously, the information in this book is also appropriate for domestic partnerships, civil unions, and commitment ceremonies, second marriages and vow renewals as well.

And in consideration of the many same-sex marriages that take place I have tried to use the term "The Couple" in place of the usual "bride and groom "as often as possible. After all, Love is Love—no matter *where, when* or *with whom* you find it!

Also, please remember that since both you and your partner will have to give rehearsal and reception speeches, I ask you to consider the other books in *The Wedding Series* when planning *your* speeches for these events. And don't forget that others have to make speeches, too. *YOUR Wedding Speech Made Easy: The "How-to" Guide for the Father of the Bride, the Best Man . . . and Everyone Else!* makes a great gift!

Okay, So What *IS* "The Tao of the Vow"?

Without going into the ancient Chinese philosophy expounded by the legendary Lao Tzu ("the Old Philosopher") around the late 4th Century BCE, (*whew*!) it simply means to find the perfect vow for *you*—in your own, personal voice; and spoken from your heart.

"Tao" (or "Dao") is a Chinese word often translated as "the way," "the path" or the "essential process." This essential process toward your vows is given in the text along with supplementary materials to help you navigate the potholes, pebbles, and boulders that will strew your path.

Path or road is a common metaphor for life's journey: "The long road ahead . . ." "the path to success . . ." "May the road rise up to meet you . . ." and so on. But though a thousand will begin the same path to their vows, each path is uniquely their own.

This book is *your* "road map" to The Way to your vows.

One common Taoist saying is *"A journey of ten thousand miles begins with a single step."* And you, dear reader, have taken that important first step by reading this book.

For you, the journey is not only the destination in and of itself, but the final destination is a Happily Ever After, Forever!

This journey is *not* about putting a few random thoughts on paper and speaking them at your wedding ceremony. There are plenty of other books that show you how to do that.

The Tao of the Vow allows you the opportunity to find within yourself the way to focus, to contemplate, to organize and record your thoughts, and to find your true poetic nature—in *every* sense of the word.

As you travel the path to your perfect vows, my hope is that you will not let me put words in your mouth, but rather that you will discover the words that flow from your heart.

Follow these simple steps, tread carefully but confidently, and find the depths of love, understanding and commitment you may not even realize you possess.

As Lao Tzu wrote:

"Knowing others shows wisdom;
Knowing yourself shows enlightenment."
—*Tao te Ching* Chapter 33

Note: I ask you to please read carefully and be certain you understand the essential processes presented here. The steps you learn can be applied to *any contemplation, writing and public speaking you might do,* not just your vows. The techniques, seriousness, and focus you will put into writing and delivering your vows will certainly be applicable beyond the scope of this book. I urge you to use this knowledge to your advantage.

So, What *IS* a Wedding Vow?

A Little Bit of History

"Vow" comes from the Latin and means to "vote" or make a solemn statement. Vows or pledges of commitment and mutual protection have been made between both individuals and between groups throughout history.

In the context of a wedding, a vow is a sincere promise and a sacred obligation—even if it is given in a secular ceremony. A vow is a public pledge of trust between the couple, and the words spoken should be carefully considered and understood before being pronounced. The vow solemnizes the marriage and is viewed as a binding covenant between the partners.

Most ceremonies, both religious and civil, usually include traditional vows, or a paraphrase of them, that have now become standards, such as those from the Book of Common Prayer:

". . . To have and to hold from this day forward, for better, for worse, for richer, for poorer, in sickness, and in health, to love and to cherish, till death us do part."

Though these are certainly cherished and beautifully worded vows that "cover all the bases" it can be said they are incomplete because they have become *too* generic. Though a tradition for hundreds of years, they do not include any *personal* sentiments and therefore lack a specific personality that makes the wedding vow unique to each couple and their special day.

I do not advocate forsaking the traditional vows altogether. However, writing a vow about your belief in and commitment to both each other and your future together will help you better understand the importance of married life. Writing your own vows forces you to think deeply about yourself, your partner and the future.

These personal vows are a brief, simply worded statement of faith, trust, hope and love between the couple. Many couples prefer to exchange them *before or after* the standard vows, instead of replacing them altogether. It is a "best of both worlds" approach that mixes the modern personal touch with the time-honored traditional.

However, you must check with your officiant to be certain that your personal vows are allowed at all. Some religious traditions hold that marriage is a sacrament and only the prescribed words from their particular book of service are allowed to be spoken by the officiant and The Couple.

But, even if you are NOT allowed to say your personal vows during your wedding ceremony, you can *still write your vows* and simply include them in your wedding speech! It is common today for *both* partners to make a brief speech at the reception and this would be the perfect time to state your personal vows.

In fact, even if you *are* able to include them at the wedding ceremony, you can repeat them as part of your wedding speech. After all, there will probably be people at your reception who weren't at the wedding. Besides, I'm certain neither you nor your new spouse would mind hearing them again!

Hey, do what you want; after all, this is *your* wedding, so if tradition just isn't working for you, *create a tradition of your own!*

Note: For help writing your wedding speeches, I once again suggest the other books in *The Wedding Series*.

An Extremely Brief History of The Wedding Vow

People have always "married" throughout time. That is to say, had children together, stayed together, and generally supported each other. However, families usually arranged the marriage and it was more often than not one of mutual benefit between families than it was of love between The Couple. The idea of marrying for romantic love is a rather recent concept.

The Couples declarations of commitment to their marriage and the promises they made personally to each other—if any—were often quite different from the traditions we have today.

Many believe that our modern concept of wedding vows originated in ancient Rome, though some argue it's really ancient Greece. (After all, it seems the Greeks thought of *everything* first!)

There were two classes of Roman society and each had differing arrangements for marriage.

The lower class (the plebs) consisted mostly of skilled and unskilled workers, artisans, and shopkeepers who had little monies, inheritance or property to worry about so they arranged a marriage by simple consensus. A father would take his daughter (women were considered chattel, the personal property of the father or eldest male in the family) to the house of the man she was to marry and the couple would both speak aloud their consent to the marriage and their promise (vow) to regard each other as husband and wife. This witnessed mutual agreement was considered a "free" or common law marriage.

However, the more wealthy class (the patricians) *did* have money, inheritance, and property to protect and a spoken agreement wasn't seen as sufficient. But, even with the patricians, women were often instruments for mutual alliances, with romance and love playing no real role in the decision to allow a marriage.

The marriage partners had to sign a document, before witnesses, declaring both their consent to marriage and their property rights; thus ensuring any offspring would be legitimate heirs. Since this vow was in writing and this public declaration was now legally binding—their marriage was official in the eyes of the Roman law. (The Romans customarily kissed each other "to seal the deal" for a contract so this may be where we get the traditional "first kiss" between husband and wife.)

Jumping through history to the medieval period, people still married in "common law," but the church increasingly insisted that the union be recognized by them, and through them, "in the eyes of God." Thus, pledges and vows made before a member of the clergy were considered both legally and spiritually were binding. These ceremonies were usually performed within the churchyard or just outside of the church door. (While the wealthy and upper class married *inside* the church, it was only much later that "common folk" were allowed to do so.)

To codify the actual wedding rite, the Church of England—formed after King Henry VIII's break with the Roman Catholic Church in 1534—compiled the Book of Common Prayer in 1549. And it is from this book and its revisions that we get the most common and traditional vows used today: "I take thee to be my wedded wife, to have and to hold from this day forward . . ."

A last word on wedding words

I have no doubt that you have heard, will soon hear or have used these wedding–related words, so you might as well know a little bit about their origins.

"Troth"—to give in truth—is an archaic word meaning to pledge or to give truthfully. When given in a be*troth*al, you were be*troth*ed: truly promised in marriage.

"Marriage" is Middle English, from the Old French *marier* which itself derives from the Latin word *maritare,* but all mean, "to wed."

"Wedding" comes from the Old English word "wed" which means "a solemn promise," such as what a king might say, "I am wedded to this trade agreement." In a marriage ceremony, the ring given to the bride showed that the husband would honor his pledge, and symbolized the act of giving that promise, the "wed-ing" ("wedding").

The English word "matrimony" comes to us from the Latin word *matrimonium,* which derives from the Latin word *mater* or "mother." This implies the main reason for the marriage: to have legitimate children who could, therefore, continue the line and receive an inheritance.

"Bridal" may have originated from the "bride's ale" brewed for and drunk by The Couple at the wedding.

"Nuptials," which means "pertaining to marriage," has been used since the mid-16th Century and comes from the Latin *nuptialis.*

Oh, and by the way, "wedlock" comes from Old English, meaning the marriage vow in action and thus the state of marriage—and *not* that you're <u>locked</u> in a marriage!

We Begin Our Journey on The Tao of the Vow

I know that this is a once in a lifetime thing (even a *second* marriage only happens once in a lifetime) and you may think that you need to be a writer or poet to write your vows, but that isn't true. Just follow the path. After all, while you may not have their writing experience, you *have* experienced the same emotions they have and you *do* have an innate poetic nature. You are human, aren't you?

"Okay," you say, *"but what about . . ."*

I'm sure you have a lot of questions to ask.

"Should we write the vows together and each of us recites the same *vow?"*

"Or should we each have our own, original vow to say?"

"How long should our vows be?"

"What should *we say?"*

"Heck, I'm not sure we have a clue <u>what</u> we're going to say!"

Don't worry! You *can* do this!

"Water [your dreams] with optimism and solutions and you will cultivate success. Always be on the lookout for ways to turn a problem into an opportunity for success."

In this case, your dream is to follow the path and write your perfect vows. So, how do you begin?

As with an actual walk down a path, you put one foot in front of the other and continue to advance. In other words: step-by-step. ("*A journey of ten thousand miles . . .*" remember?)

We are going to set a path to the perfect vows for *you*, unique *to* you. It may be rocky at times, but it *will* get you there.

You will learn how to navigate the landscape; how to stay on the path and keep moving forward. And if you stumble? Just get back up, brush yourself off and take the next step.

The entire process is a means to achieve some personal enlightenment so that when you do pronounce your vows (either/or your personal and traditional vows) you follow the simple precept:

"Say what you mean and mean what you say."

As we have discussed, your vow is a solemn oath, a sworn pledge, a promise that you swear to keep. So take your time and follow the path.

Again: **Don't worry!** You *can* do this!

Are you ready to create vows that are as unique and special as you and your love for your partner? The way to your vows begins now. It's time to take that first step on your journey. So, take a deep breath and let's get started!

Note: Throughout the book, all italicized quotes are from the *Tao te Ching* or other philosophic Taoist texts.

Also, I have put several blank pages for your notes in the book, at the Appendices and at the end of the book.

Your First Steps on the Path:

Create a Plan of Action

"One is born into certain relationships and as a result, has certain duties"

"Action should be taken before a thing has made its appearance; order should be secured before disorder has begun."

The first step on your path is for you and your partner to sit down and discuss *how* you will approach writing your vows. You both have a lot to consider.

This is the time to be open and honest with each other regarding your vows. This is the time to "cuss and discuss" *everything* about your vows. And, since *both* of you need to agree on your ideas for what your vows should be, you should begin each of these 10 plan suggestions with the phrase "an agreement."

The following guidelines are some of the things your plan should include:

+ An agreement that each of you will make an *equal* commitment to the process of writing the vows

+ An agreement to allow some time for both of you to reflect on your relationship now and going forward before you first meet to discuss your vows

+ An agreement on a time limit for your vows: two to three minutes is usual—that's about 160 to 360 words long; you're *really* pushing it at four minutes (save the rest for your wedding speech at the reception!) But then again, it is your wedding! So if you agree on a one-minute vow or a five-minute vow, so be it! And remember, what is important is *what* you say, not how many words it takes you to say it!

+ An agreement on whether you will write the vows together and each recite the *same* vow

+ An agreement on whether to write your *separate* vows together and discuss them, or write them *separately* and keep them a surprise

+ An agreement on whether or not you will each share the same beginning of your vows, such as "I vow (promise, pledge) to . . ."

+ An agreement on whether or not to include certain promises, like in the traditional vows where you both agree to the *same* promises (love, honor, cherish, etc.) and, if so, an agreement as to what these promises should be

+ An agreement to keep the vows conversational and not overly dramatic

+ An agreement on your vows general tone—humorous, serious, poetic, romantic, etc.—because you do not want one person's ideas of vows to be a comic monolog and the others to be deadly serious—but to respect the individuality of each and allow each of your personalities to show in your vows

+ An agreement that you will both meet periodically and talk about the progress you are making . . .

+ but with an agreed upon deadline to make certain the vows are done and not something hurriedly cobbled together by one or the both of you

So, have you two "cussed and discussed?" Did you argue a little? Have you two finally agreed, and kissed and made up? Then, Congratulations! You have both taken the first few steps on the way to your vows!

Okay, now that you have agreed on what to do, you can move on to the second part.

The Rocky Road Ahead:

Writing Your Vows

Step One—Research: No Rocks, just a few Potholes

Note: Do NOT throw away any of the lists you will make. Each one will have topics and phrases you can use for the rehearsal and/or reception speeches; as well as things you can write in the letter you planned to give your spouse on your first anniversary! (You *did* plan to do that, *didn't you*?)

"Ordinary men hate solitude. But the Master uses it, accepting his aloneness, realizing he is one with the whole universe."

How do you begin your research? It's easy: simply think about your beloved!

Just sit down in a quiet place, where there are no real distractions (you'll need to have a productive mindset). Perhaps lower the lights, put on some of your favorite music (sound turned down) and take a pen and several blank pieces of paper, and simply *think* about your intended. Accept your aloneness and allow yourself to relax and to think, to *simply remember*.

Meditate, contemplate, concentrate—allow yourself a state of mindfulness.

(*Okay, there is a little more to it than that, so read on.*)

. . .

"There is nothing in the world as soft and weak as water, and yet for attacking things that are firm and strong there is nothing that can be more powerful..."

Why? Because water goes over, under, around or through any obstacles. As they said in the '60s: GO WITH THE FLOW!

Just let your memories flow! Let them flow like water, over, under and around any obstructions. Think visually; picture your intended. *Brainstorm*! Don't be deterred.

What you will do is solve the problem of what to write by using a creative process to generate ideas. As the memories flow, you will make associations between the image and your feelings. Put these visualizations into words or phrases and make a note of them.

You will be using both your conscious, voluntary memory as you *try* to recall things about your beloved, and your subconscious, involuntary memory, finding thoughts or memories coming willy-nilly as your memories flow. In other words, something you think about and write down evokes yet another thought. It may be a phrase, a piece of poetry, song lyrics—but all are linked by your memory.

Trust me, this process works. It certainly worked for the French novelist Marcel Proust who wrote about "forgotten" memories evoked by dipping a *Madeleine* cake in a cup of tea in his reallly looong novel—7 volumes!—*A la recherché du temps perdue,* often translated as *Remembrance of Things Past.*

Although many people will simply make a list of words (and that's okay), my suggestion would be for you to use a topic mapping technique, like clustering and branching or "mind-mapping."

Topic mapping is a technique where, in this case, you take a blank piece of paper, draw a circle in the middle and label it "vows," and then write the words, idea or phrase your memories bring beside the circle, then circling these. Any words, ideas or phrases that *these* words then inspire are written near *that* circle and then they too are circled, and so on. Use a line to connect each circle to the word that inspired it.

Picture it this way, the "vows" circle is the hub of your wheel of ideas. The words you wrote around this and circled, are connected to this main hub by "spokes,"(your lines) and the words you wrote around *these* words and circled (becoming smaller "hubs"), are connected to *these* other words by more "spokes" and on and on. It's like the "spider diagram" in mathematics.

Still not certain what topic mapping is? Look it up on the web. There are plenty of articles and diagrams to check out.

This technique will make organizing and prioritizing easier when you need to edit what you've written. And these techniques are applicable to both writings and speeches you may need to give in the future. Learn it once and use it forever!

An Example of Cluster and Branching

Note: This can be used as either a list format or "Tree" (as shown) or as a more traditional "mind-map" with the VOWS as the center hub and the other words, ideas or phrases radiating from it.

```
              (Admire)
             /
            /    (Respect)
          /   /         \
         /   /         (Tolerance) - - - (understanding)
       (Honor)
      /
(VOWS)      (All You Do) - - - (how you make me
     \            /                  feel)
      \          /
       (Cherish)
            \
          (Our Time Together)
```

'VOWS' is the first word (the main idea or center hub); in this example that word has made you associate the words 'HONOR' and 'CHERISH' with it (First Level). *Those* words led you to associate 'HONOR' with *'ADMIRE'* and *'RESPECT'* (Second Level) and 'CHERISH' with *'ALL YOU DO'* and *'OUR TIME TOGETHER'* (Second Level). *'RESPECT'* is associated with '**Tolerance**' (Third Level), which leads to '**understanding**' (Fourth Level) and so on.

. . .

Every mental image you conjure will help bring feelings about your love to the surface, so it should be a simple task to skim them and write them on your paper, right?

NOPE!

Believe it or not, this can be very hard to do. How do you put your memories and your feelings into words? How do you express what is in your heart? How do you articulate what you truly feel?

At this point, you'll probably think to yourself, "How can I *tell* my partner *how* I love them? I just *do*!

"'I love you' is too plain. *'I love you with a passion beyond words'* is too poetic, and is that really *me*—is that what *I* would *really* say?"

Let's face it: Love is impossible to put into words. How can you define it? How can you describe what it means to *you*? Writers and poets have tried (and failed) for centuries! A kiss is far more eloquent than mere words; so how can you reduce to mere words the passion that your partner creates in you?

Well, to take this step along the path you must rely on the stereotype of the psychiatrist. You know, the patient says something and the psychiatrist asks, "How does *that* make you feel?"

Think about your beloved and ask yourself, "How *does* he/she make me feel?"

Do his/her eyes show a loving soul? Does his/her smile lighten your heart? What effect does he/she have on you? How has he/she changed your life?

Relax and slowly take that step—just think about him/her and how he/she makes you feel.

As you begin to know, just jot down *everything* about him/her that comes to mind. Quantity over quality at this point! There are NO wrong answers here! Neatness doesn't even count. Just let the words flow! Fill in your list or topic map!

This brainstorming should be easy and certainly not a chore; after all, The Love of Your Life should always be on your mind anyway!

So, RELAX! Don't complicate things. Don't think about him/her too hard. Just let it happen! Just let it flow!

This process may take some time; so don't be in a rush. A few minutes today, a few tomorrow and you'll do fine!

Note: It is *very important* that you DO NOT EDIT YOURSELF. YOU *MUST* IGNORE SELF-CENSORSHIP! Just write. You will be tempted to read what you have jotted down and erase or revise it. Do NOT give into that temptation! No self-criticism is allowed right now.

Did you write the same thing a couple times? Spelled something wrong? It's okay. Don't worry. Right now, just write.

If it seems that you just can't come up with anything (*shame on you!*) you can refer to the "Words and Phrases Cheat Sheet" in the Appendices for inspiration.

. . .

"Love is a decision - not an emotion!"

Perhaps you are feeling self-conscious about writing these impressions of your beloved. You may think they are clichéd, insubstantial, too ordinary—and you may be right! But at this point, that's okay; so don't worry, you're doing fine.

It is very true that you can't really know anyone else until you know yourself.

And you can't really know yourself until you know the people *you choose* to associate with.

And <u>*you*</u> decided to fall in love with this particular person!

Therefore, it follows that by contemplating your feelings about your partner, you will uncover a truer sense of *your own self.* You become more mindful of just whom *you* are.

Now is the time to be totally subjective and sentimental. Don't judge yourself. You decided to love this one person, so be honest and tell yourself "*Why?*"

Write one or two words. A few simple phrases. That's all. There is no need elaboration at this step. Just make your list/map.

. . .

"What if I have the mental image," you ask, *"but I just can't find the feelings? I know I have them, I just can't find them now that I need them!"*

Well, don't panic; you've just hit a pothole on your path.

If you're having trouble getting started, try these thought starters:

Questions to Ask Yourself

+ If someone had never met him/her how would you describe him/her?

+ What adjectives or simple phrases best identify your beloved?

+ How did you meet; what were the circumstances?

+ What attracted you to him/her?

+ When was the first time you realized you loved him/her? What made you realize it?

+ Think of everything that he/she means to you; how have *you* changed because of his/her influence and love for you?

+ What do you share in common—not just traits, but outlooks, activities, tastes in food, entertainment, life goals, etc.?

+ Do you share a favorite song or poem that has a lyric or phrase that describes him/her?

+ Do you share a favorite joke and sense of humor? What else do you share that him/her "fun" to be with?

+ What have been the highlights *and* lowlights of your relationship? How did you both get through them?

+ How did he/she support you when/if you've had a crisis since you've been together?

+ Just what things make him/her such a wonderful match to you?

Simply put and most importantly:

WHY is he/she "The One?"

What makes him/her the "ONLY ONE?"

. . .

Some Topics to Include

Now that you have started a rough list of words and phrases about the person you are going to marry, you're out of the pothole and back on the path!

It's time to think about your relationship *after* you're married.

(*It is my sincere hope you have already discussed this with your partner! If not, my book* Questions for Couples: What to Ask Before You Say "I Do" *is a great place to start.*)

Your vows should include some statements of positive intent for your life together and not just a declaration of your love. These should be promises beyond the traditional ". . . in sickness and in health . . ." etc.

Here are some thought starters on topics you might consider incorporating in your vows:

The ***Acceptance*** of each other; that you are two different, unique people. True individuals accept each other as they are and celebrate their individuality.

There must be ***Communication*** between each of you; always keeping that communication open and honest.

When you talk, you should always ***Discuss,*** never browbeat; and you should confer with each other on any decision affecting the both you.

You should ***Listen*** to each other; truly hearing what the other has to say.

There must be ***Understanding and forgiveness*** to keep the little things from becoming big things.

You must exercise ***Tolerance*** of and for each other quirks and idiosyncrasies—allowing each other time alone and "breathing room" if needed.

You must realize that there must be ***Effort*** expended because marriage takes work.

That you must recognize that your definition of love will change as you *both* grow and change.

That you both must ***Maintain*** a good nature and sense of humor.

That you should ***Learn*** from each other and your life together; and as you grow—grow *together.*

Forgive each other; kiss and make up; say "I Love You!" every night before going to sleep and every morning when you awaken.

Appreciate all that you are as a person, all that you can give to your partner and your relationship, and all that you share in your life together.

. . .

Still need something else? Think about the **basic promises** that are in the traditional vows—"to love, honor, cherish; in sickness and health; for richer or poorer," etc.—and reword them in "your speak," a personal reiteration.

Having to restate them in your own words will give you a chance to think about these particular promises and what they mean to both you and your partner.

. . .

As you write these, remember: Simple expressions of love and hope are always best.

In other words: When it comes to your vows, poetry is great but honesty is greater. For now, just write what you honestly feel. You will compose your simple jottings into "poetry" later down the path.

Here are some more ideas to help you:

Many vows will include *how your life has changed*, such as "my life has changed for the better since I met you," "I can never love another now that you are mine," "I was lost before I met you, and now I'd be lost without you," and the like. You can include these too.

You can also *create a laundry list of the things you like, indeed* love, *about each other*. "I love the way your cheeks blush when . . ." "I love you sparkling eyes, your soft lips, your . . ." "I love your scent as you walk by; your hair in the gentle breeze; the way you smile . . ."

You might also write about your *plans and hopes for the future* together. These may include phrases such as "I'll share all my dreams with you as we go forward . . ." "Should we be so blessed, I can think of no better (mother/father) . . ." "There is nothing we cannot accomplish together." etc.

Look within yourself and then look over your list. Have you added what flowed as you thought about both your partner and your future together? Can you still add anything? If you are not sure, don't worry; you'll have time to re-read what you have written and revise it later.

. . .

Need More Help? Don't forget the Appendices in the back of this book. Perhaps you'll find inspiration in some of the famous quotes about love and marriage, or in the "Cheat Sheets" with vow keywords and phrases—in fact, *especially* the Words and Phrases Cheat Sheet! Perhaps inspiration will come by reading the traditional vows and some of the more contemporary ones listed there.

Please Don't! But ya really gotta . . .

I sincerely hope you're not, but if you are *really* stuck, and want the ultimate cheat, I guess you can recite the vows I've already written in the Appendices. However, these should truly only be used as inspirations, mere "starting off points." However, if you must use them, you really should try to personalize them, *at the very least*!

Careful, though, for this is truly cheating both your partner *and yourself*! It's starting a path, deciding it is too hard, and phoning a taxi to carry you the rest of the way. Sure, you get to your final destination but—oh my!—you have missed so much along the way!

Okay, there you have it! At last, it's time to create your list. Now that you have read all the tips and suggestions, it's up to you! Just write—but Think, Remember, and write what your Memory makes you feel!

. . .

When you have finally finished, I'll bet that your paper has more items on it than you thought it would—but it really doesn't matter if you have 5 items or 50 items as long as they are true reflections of your thoughts about your partner and your future together. Look at your paper; understand what you have done.

I know that at times it might have seemed like pulling teeth because it *is* so very difficult to put into words all the thoughts you have and the emotions you feel—but you did it! You should be very proud of yourself!

A Half-Step Forward

"Have you the patience to wait until the mud settles and the water is clear?"

Okay. You have a list of jottings that seem to be in no particular order and seem to make no sense. It might be a mind-map—but it looks like a map to nowhere! It's like looking through muddy water—*you can't see the bottom*!

So, what's next?

Now is when your work really begins, but remember: it *is* a labor of love! Even so, as with any venture, you will get out of it only what you put into it. I know that you may sometimes feel that this is a waste of commitment, time and energy; but that is not so. If you need to, take a day and forget about your vows. Let the mud settle a little. Maintain a positive mental attitude, because when you come back to them is when you must buckle down and apply yourself so that you don't let your partner write a beautiful set of vows and all you can do is say "Ditto!"

Are you ready to start? You now need to read your list or topic map *carefully* and see if you have duplicated anything. Maybe it is a whole phrase you've written several times or you see that you have used the same word in different phrases.

If you find these, *neatly* write that phrase or word on a *separate* sheet of paper. On your original sheet, *lightly* cross through the things you've recopied (don't obliterate them).

These duplicates are what make him/her *singular* in your mind. In other words, these are the things that *you* consider most important in your view of your partner—that's *why* you wrote them several times!

Looking at the other things you've written: does anything seem "out of place?" maybe a little "too far afield?" Reread these and if they still strike you as too different, strike them through, but *lightly* so. These were probably spurious, random feelings and are usually not worthy of further consideration. However, it is possible that you will need to come back to them!

List the remaining things from your jottings on this new piece of paper and you will have a rough example of your thoughts and ideas about your partner and your relationship.

And guess what? You've completed your first revision—your first edit!

(Even with this, though, I'll bet that your list/map is much longer than you first thought it would be—and that's great!)

"Let (the muddy water) be still and it will gradually become clear."

"The world belongs to those who let go."

What to do next? Take your new, neat list and . . . put it in a drawer somewhere. As my friends from New Jersey say, "*fuggedaboudit*!"

That's right: Let your brainstorm subside! Go out and walk the dog, play golf, go to work (ugh!). Do something—anything—to take your mind off the list and let a couple of days pass before you look at it again.

Why? As with any problem that you "can't wrap your mind around," just "sleep on it!" (*Who said clichés are worthless*?)

What you are doing is allowing you mind to subconsciously consider what you wrote and what may be missing. It could be a thought or feeling that hadn't initially occurred to you, or it could be one of those random things you previously crossed out.

Though I know you may be tempted, *don't* sneak a peek at the list/map! Just relax and let your mind do its thing.

When you *do* look at what you wrote a few days later, the "muddy water of your thoughts" will be clear and you may note that what seemed to be random now makes sense. Also, you may wind up adding words or phrases that are missing, and you'll wonder why you didn't think of them in the first place.

What you will have done is look at your list/map with a fresh set of eyes (and a clearer mind). And, trust me, it is always important to see things through "fresh eyes!"

The Organization of Unrelated Ideas: Stepping Carefully Around the Potholes

With fresh eyes and clear vision, the time has come to *really look* at what you have written and to organize it.

You need this second revision to turn your "raw data" into a useable format for your vows.

This time, you need to look for potential groupings and possible categories from what you have written. Try to arrange what you have into several broad groupings, like Love, Commitment, Togetherness, etc. (If you used topic mapping you have already done a lot of this.)

Once categorized, if you find that you have only single words, try to turn them into a brief phrase. "*Understanding*" can become "you accept me for me" or "you accept me as I am."

As you read these more organized words and phrases you may find that what stands out among your list is a rehashing of the standard vows, just in your own words—and there's no shame in that. After all, these vows have been used for centuries and you have personalized and customized them.

. . .

Now the hard part: Take the phrases that you have grouped and write them into rough sentences.

Don't worry about sentence structure or grammar right now. Just write your sentences and keep editing the words or phrases into something that is useable.

And what if it seems that you have just a jumble of clichés? Well, a cliché is simply an over-used and, therefore, too familiar, word or phrase. However, that does NOT mean that it is inappropriate to use! A cliché became a cliché because it is so perfectly appropriate that *everyone* uses it. If the cliché truly describes how you feel, it's up to you to either embrace it or avoid it The following may help you find a way to "rethink" a cliché.

Here are some examples of phrases turned into sentences:

"You're always in my heart" can become "Wherever I am by myself, I am never alone because you're always with me; always in my heart."

or

"I love your smile" can become "To start my day and before going to sleep; when I'm happy or not so happy, I see your smile and my life just becomes better."

(*Sappy? You bet! Ain't nothing wrong with that*!)

Don't worry about the order your sentences are in, or how they sound when you read them. Remember, this is only your *first draft,* so play with it and don't expect perfection. You only want to express *your* best effort and *your* sincerest thoughts about the one you love.

So, what have you written? Ten sentences? Twenty? Too many, you think? Don't worry—they'll soon be pared down.

Note: Now your ideas are categorized and written in sentences, but not yet completely organized into a speech. It is important to remember that when you write your vows, *you are writing a speech.* After all, your vows will not be read on paper but will be spoken.

. . .

If you and your partner are going to write your vows together, you will do this second edit *with* him/her. If you are writing separately, look at your list/map and think about the promises you would make to him/her. Pretend he/she is there and think about how he/she would react.

Help Along the Way

Whether you and your partner have written this first draft together or separately, it is best to have someone else take a look at it. (Obviously, you do not want your partner to be that person if you are writing separate vows.)

You might show them to a trusted friend or family member. Whomever is chosen, always ask them for honest criticism.

Because they see you and your partner from a different perspective and aren't caught up in the immediacy of your relationship, they can usually offer helpful suggestions concerning your vows. ("Fresh eyes," remember?)

You might also want an older married friend or family member to have a look at your list and discuss with you what married life is *really* like. Their experience will be helpful well beyond any comments they make about your vow list and will certainly give you a few new thoughts about promises to make.

In fact, even if you and your partner *are* writing together, "fresh eyes" and a different perspective would still help, so find a mutual friend to look at what you've done so far.

It is important that when a third party looks over your draft and comments, that you do NOT allow any critical comments to discourage you, nor should you take them personally. That is why I suggest that you have these initial comments (and, indeed, all future revisions) reviewed by a trusted friend or family member because they will only have *your* best interests at heart.

To be honest, ego always plays a part in any creative endeavor, so you probably *will* feel put off by any criticism but don't let your ego become a stumbling block to *your* creative effort. Take these honest criticisms, suggestions, insights, and comments that you have been given and *rewrite* some of the sentences on your list or broaden or eliminate categories.

Take your time and maybe you too will find a few things that you can tweak. Ain't no such thing as "perfect!"

Once you have these vows *roughly* edited it's time for the next step: better organization and the final edit.

The Scissors Come Out!

"On earth, we can see beauty as beauty only because there is (the contrast of) ugliness."

All right. You've looked over what you have written and a third-party has offered constructive criticism. Now is the time for your proverbial scissors come out and you snip, snip, snip.

In other words, EDITING! This is almost always a stumbling block because now (and especially *if* you are writing your vows together) is when you eliminate much of what's taken you all that time to write.

"*WHAT!*" you ask. "*How can I possibly bring myself to eliminate so many wonderful expressions of love and commitment?*"

It isn't easy, but it *must* be done. If you don't, you may have a twenty-minute vow! Besides, you can always incorporate the leftovers into your wedding speech. (*You haven't forgotten that you have to give one, have you?*)

What you are looking for now is a final few sentences that honestly distil your thoughts and feelings. After all, you have both agreed to a word or time limit for your vows anyway, so you're just adhering to protocol.

Look through your list for a few carefully chosen thoughts or vows that <u>*you*</u> consider *most essential*.

Look over your sentences and read each one aloud. Perhaps you'll hear yourself saying the same kind of thing, just in a different way, or you'll hear the same word repeated over and over. This may mean that you can edit a little more. Reread each sentence and choose the ones you think best convey what truly mean to say. Rewrite others as needed. However, always carefully consider what you are doing and what you are choosing.

One technique to edit and shorten your list is to <u>circle or highlight</u> what you *most* want to say. Then <u>underline</u> the things you'd *like* to say; and finally, draw a *light* pencil line through the rest (you don't want to make them illegible; remember, you might need to reconsider these later or for your wedding speech).

The items you circled or highlighted items are the most important vow ideas—as *you've* chosen them; and the others are secondary, though still important to you.

Write the sentences you've *circled/highlighted* on a new sheet of paper, followed by the ones you've <u>underlined</u>: These are now your newly edited vow items.

Lastly, look at *this* list and see if it needs further editing. Maybe, maybe not.

Now, organize *these* sentences. Make them coherent; make them flow. Look in the Appendices for some ideas on the structure. (You'll learn a little more in the next chapter.)

Just Edit! Trust me—it's really okay to do. The key is to rewrite your final draft until *you* are satisfied with it. Ask yourself: Have I included what I really intend to say? *Am I sure*?

When *you* have made every consideration and are satisfied, your vows will have been edited, shortened and the best you can make them. They have come from within your deepest thoughts and feelings and emerged on the printed page. You have navigated through the rocks!

As you have walked the path thus far, I'll bet that you have gained some insight into yourself, your partner and your future together. After all, you have considered things a person normally wouldn't really think about, let alone contemplate and commit to paper, so:

Congratulations!

Note: As before, if you are writing your vows together and planning to recite the *same* vows, you need to meet and share what you have. Either hand each other the vow list you have made or read it aloud. Each of you can then comment on what you think is best on each other's list and what you both agree can be discarded. This is when you again "cuss and discuss" to make these custom vows the best they can be as a representation of *the both of you*. After all, since you have decided to recite the *same* vows to each other, you certainly need to agree on them.

If you are each writing individual vows *and* wish to keep them a surprise until the wedding, you obviously cannot share them with your intended.

Whichever way, you will once again need to ask your trusted friend or family member to read and comment on these newly edited vows.

Step Two—Formatting Your Speech -A Smooth Stretch

Note: The examples given are roughly about a minute or so in length when spoken . . . *way too short*, since most wedding vows are usually a full two or three minutes long. These are just suggestions for organization of your edited, ordered sentences. YOUR vows should conform to your agreed upon word/time limit.

After adjusting this draft of your speech, if you have more on your list than you can use, remember, you can always use these "leftovers" in your reception or first-anniversary speech.

Before you can put your vows into a speech, you need to know the two basic types of vow structures. This will help you decide how best to organize *your* vows. Let's look at both of them.

The ***First Format*** is the basic structure of *any* speech:

Introduction

Body (Vows, in this case)

Conclusion

This is an example of a *very* simple vow following the First Format:

> "Because of you (name), I have found a love I never thought I would find. Your love is a gift and you have given me more than I can ever give *you* in a lifetime.
>
> "I will try to, though, by pledging my undying love for you alone; to always be an honest friend; to take care of you in good times and bad, and to share with you all that we may encounter.
>
> "You are my life, my dearest (name), and I vow to love you forever and ever."

(That's less than 100 words!)

The ***Second Format*** is a less rigid, and more modern, free form statement about your feelings for your partner and is usually spoken *before* you recite the traditional vows.

This is an example of the Second Format:

"Time, for me, began when I met you. From that first second, I loved you. And I shall until my last. Every moment we are together, Time seems to fade, to stand still. YOU fill my every second; and still, Time passes . . . all too swiftly.

Before I know it, the seconds have turned to minutes, to hours, into days. I am lost in Time . . . I am lost in YOU!

"Time began with you and though Time will always pass, as it must, every moment of my life is filled with you; every tick of the clock is an eternity of love shared with you. And as the hands of the clock ever turn in a circle, its movement is like the wedding ring I will wear symbolizing my eternal, unending Love, now and through all Time."

(That's about 134 words! You could certainly add more.)

Remember, chances are you will still use the "traditional vows," as many religious and civil authorities require certain wording for doctrinal and/or legal reasons. Arrange your personal vows into whichever style you prefer and try not to duplicate anything in these "traditional vows" unless it is a personal reiteration. That way you are not excluding what your faith (or the law) requires you to say; you're only enhancing it.

Should I Include Humor in my Vows?
(Be Careful of the Quicksand!)

One big question that is often asked is "*Should we include humor in our vows?*" Well, did you *both* agree to it? Or, do you think it appropriate as a reflection of your individual personalities?

I caution that if you <u>do</u> choose to include humor, that you *please be careful*!

Sometimes humor is a welcome guest on such a solemn occasion. Other times it is an unwelcome intruder.

So, if you do decide to use humor, *please* do so carefully! Make it *light* and *short*.

Some examples of "humor" I've heard include such "gems" as:

"I promise to *always* listen to your advice . . . and occasionally follow it."

His view of domestic life:

"I promise to always put the seat down in the bathroom."

Bad puns:

"I'm glad you *joined* me . . . I'd come apart without you in my life."

On sports: "I promise to love you through good times, when the (favorite team's name) are winning and bad times when they are losing . . ."

Sci-Fi buffs:

"I feel that I've known you all my life; as though I met you a long, long time ago, in a galaxy far, far away. I love you so much I'd fight a Star Wars to keep you mine."

"My heart is like a TARDIS—seemingly so small on the outside, but infinite on the inside."

Funny? Chuckle-worthy? Ummmm, *maybe*. But if you have both agreed on a touch of humor, it is only important that you *both* think it's cute . . . even if the audience groans.

Remember, though, just don't make your humor too "inside." Allow your audience to share the joke.

Step Three—Writing Your Vows: a bumpy stretch—not rocks, just pebbles.

(Okay, I lied! Maybe a lot of rocks!)

"The path into the light seems dark, the path forward seems to go back, the direct path seems long..."

Now that you have your final list of vows and know the two basic vow structures, my friend, it is up to you—this is where *your* hardest work really begins!

You and you alone, must create, craft, construct, and cobble your vow. (*Hey, I promised it would be simple, I never said it would be easy!*)

Although this is the part where you "write" your vows, in truth you have already done that. You have already taken an unorganized jumble of words and phrases, culled them into a list, edited that list and made sentences of them; edited *those* and finally put the most important ones into a rough paragraph structure! Wow! Be proud of yourself!

. . .

"Rushing into action, you fail. Forcing a project to completion, you ruin what was almost ripe…Therefore, the Master takes action by letting things take their course."

If you can, do what you did before: put your vows away and forget about them for a few days. Once again, you'll approach them with fresh eyes and a relaxed mind.

When you finally retrieve your vows, you might need to *re*organize what you have already organized! (*Crazy, ain't it*?) You have already done a basic check for coherency and flow, but now you need to double-check!

Rearrange and re-categorize 'til your heart's content. Remember, they must be like water—that is, the ideas must have a natural flow.

Use your edited vows as your guide, but don't just string the vows together. Now is the time to care about sentence and paragraph structure.

Ask yourself the following:

"How will they *sound* when I read them aloud?"

"Do they make sense in their present order? Do they flow together naturally?" (If they don't, move them around as needed to make something that is more cohesive.)

"Do they need an introduction?"

"Have the words I've finally chosen *truly* convey what I want to say?"

(Hint: Now might be a good time to look at or re-read the Appendices and see if there is anything—a word or phrase from the "cheat sheets"—you could incorporate to help clarify or deepen your expression of love and commitment. Be sure to read the vow samples there to see if they might help you find a final organizational structure.)

Remember: As you finally organize your chosen vows, READ THEM ALOUD! You will be giving a speech and the words must flow. Novelists write differently from playwrights because their writing is read "internally," only heard by "the mind's ear." Playwrights write for their words to be spoken aloud. So you must now switch from being a novelist to a playwright! Read the vows aloud and *listen* to what you have written. Ask yourself: "Are they a true an expression of my love, and hope for our future together?"

Once again, have someone you trust read what you have written. That's right—just *read* them! You'll need to practice your delivery before you present your vows for your trusted friend to listen to. And critique how they sound.

Yes, there are several more steps along the path!

I realize this is work and real work at that. Some might even say that it's misery, but . . .

"Do not fear misery!—for happiness is found by its side!"

It's Always Best To Just Be YOU

"Must you value what others value, avoid what others avoid? How ridiculous!"

What words have you chosen to convey your sentiments? Which speech format did you choose for the vows? One, the other—or did you mix them up? Maybe you tried your own ideas. Hey, it's *your* wedding after all!

Your vows are a reflection of *you* and your deepest thoughts and feelings regarding your partner. Like the book title says, "*YOUR* perfect Wedding Vows." So, do NOT let convention compromise you!

Your vows are your personal statement and should reflect not only how you feel about your partner and your future together, but be a reflection of you as an individual.

Even so, there are a few conventions to keep in mind.

When writing your vows remember your agreed upon time limit. The majority of vows are about 2 to 3 minutes long *at most.* (By the way, if you look at your vows and say to yourself, *"Two or three minutes isn't long enough, I'll need more than that,"* do this: try and hold your breath for three minutes. You'll find three minutes is a *lot* longer than you think!) However, if you find that you need five minutes, that's okay—as long as your partner agrees. As I said before: it's *your* wedding!

The majority of English-speaking adults tend to speak between 80-120 words per minute on average, so a two-minute vow would be about 160-240 words long, a three-minute would be 240-360 words long, and so on.

Though you need to write your vows to *whatever* time or word limit you and your partner have agreed on, remember: <u>what is important is *what* you say, not *how many* words it takes you to say it!</u>

Note: When someone is nervous (as you are bound to be), they tend to speak more quickly. You can compensate for this by either having a slightly longer word count or by remembering to slow down, enunciate and pronounce each word of your vow. Adjust your writing using the appropriate Speakers Symbols. These are notes added to your speech that direct you how to speak. The most common ones are the comma (,) or slash (/), meaning to *briefly* pause; the period (.), meaning to come to a *full stop* and pause longer. If you need to pause for emphasis in the middle of a sentence, you can use a double slash (//). If you need to emphasize a word or phrase for dramatic effect, underline it. And don't forget to breathe! Take a breath at every full stop (.) or note a breath with a triple-slash (///).

When you have truly personalized this next draft, once again read what you have written *aloud*. Listen to how the words sound. Do the words flow, or are they choppy? Are both the sentence structures and grammar right? Do the tone and sentiment match what you want to say? Do the words sound like *you*—the way you *normally* talk? After all, your vows should sound like part of your natural conversation and reflect who *you* are. They should *not* sound like an academic reading a treatise on modern marriage!

Read your vows aloud to a trusted friend or family member, preferably the same one you chose to read your draft. Again, ask them for their honest feedback, and have them listen as much to your delivery as the words you have written. You know and they know that you are not an actor, so don't worry too much about your performance. (We'll discuss that later in the book).

Then, if needed, and based on the feedback, edit and rewrite *again* until you are happy with your vows—and you're certain your partner will be too!

This entire process is labor intensive. *And it should be*!

Your wedding vows should not be something cobbled together at the last minute! If you have taken your writing seriously—and, you should have!—then <u>you *must* have put forth the effort!</u> Good for you! It is not only satisfying to know that you did it, but that the vows *you have written* are endowed with your deepest feelings!

The Path has often been difficult and has certainly required a lot of your time and labor, but that should be okay because this has been a labor of Love!

Understand that:

"One can achieve happiness only by pursuing the happiness of others because it is only by forgetting about one's own happiness that one can become truly happy."

In other words, PLEASE take your time finalizing your vows. It's been a long road, strewn with obstacles . . . and you still have a way to go. Yes, you've written the vows and feel good about it—but you still have to polish your delivery. (*Sigh*!)

Now is not the time to allow yourself to become frustrated or discouraged. You've done GREAT!

Look at what you have accomplished: simple and elegant vows; written from the heart; dictated by the soul and soon to be delivered with love! <u>Be *very* proud of yourself</u>!

I know this has been a long, and at times, difficult process, but your patience *will* be rewarded: On the day you speak the vows, you'll feel satisfaction in your heart and see the smile and (probably) tears of joy on your partners face!

Note: Remember, I cannot tell you what to write, for I cannot know what is truly in your heart. I can only guide you along the path to discovering what is already there. And you've done a great job so far! Don't slow down now! My hope is that you have discovered that, in the end, editing your vows into a few brief paragraphs really wasn't the point of this at all. The journey was about your finding a way to look inside yourself and discover a deeper understanding of your feelings for the person that you are going to marry.

Delivering Your Vows:

Your Last Few Steps Along The Path

(And How to Fight the Dreaded Butterflies!)

Practicing your Vows

As I said earlier, you are not an actor. So you will have some work to do to learn how best to deliver your vows. The following are some tips and suggestions that will help.

The first thing to do is try and lose your sense of self; to live in the moment; to realize that even if you have a stadium full of people watching you, your audience is really only the person to whom you are saying your vows. Your only real audience is your "one and only."

Secondly, there are six words that will help you make a perfect delivery: PRACTICE, PRACTICE, and PRACTICE SOME MORE!

This should be your mantra: "Practice = Proficiency = Confidence = Comfort!"

On the day of your wedding, as you stand beside your partner in front of the officiant and your guests, you *WILL* be nervous! You're human. It's natural.

I have yet to meet a couple who didn't have *some* jitters. All it means is that you're just like everyone else who's ever been married. You're making a life-long commitment and that is nerve-racking. Welcome to the club!

So, How do you overcome your nerves or calm them a little?

First, try and stay calm and *Don't Worry* about it. The more you worry and fret about it, the more ingrained that worry becomes and the bigger the "fear monster" grows. You know, "self-fulfilling prophecy," "vicious circle," and all that. *Knowing* that you will be anxious will help you overcome it because you've recognized the problem—always the first step in *solving* the problem. But don't just acknowledge the problem—accept it. In fact, own it! Besides, it ain't all bad—a little nervousness will help you focus. So . . .

Learn to accept the fact that you will have some anxiety. Everyone gets butterflies in their stomachs—just ask Barbra Streisand. She admits to being exceedingly nervous before she appears on stage, even though she is a beloved and veteran performer. All the same, over the years she has gained some self-confidence.

Second, *you* can gain self-confidence, by following these tips:

You must keep everything in perspective. While it's true your vows are an *important* part of the ceremony, your vows are *just a part* of the wedding ceremony, which is *just a part* of the wedding day. There is so much going on that you really shouldn't worry about a few minutes of the whole thing.

Remember too that you have spent a great deal of time preparing your vows, so spend time practicing them. Write them down several times, saying each word to yourself as you do so. Copying them out will help you become familiar with the vows. But don't *try* to remember *everything*! Your goal is not to memorize your vows! If you strictly depend on your memory, you're liable to forget some of them and ruin the moment. Besides, you will eventually write your vows on index cards and carry them with you—just in case. Being familiar with your vows will help you *speak* your vows, rather than just read them from the note cards.

I know that you have notated your written vows with Speakers Symbols, but have you truly *listened to how you say them?* You should speak them as you would in conversation, but add a touch of drama.

Now, don't pretend you are an actor reciting some Shakespearian soliloquy—all grand eloquence, and the like; but do add some drama by emphasizing some of the words or phrases.

How about an actor's practice exercise—

Say each of the following sentences emphasizing the underlined word:

"*I* love you!"

"I *love* you!"

"I love *you*!"

"*I* love *you*!"

"*I love you*!"

Hear the differences? Now re-read your vows yet again and find where you can add a little dramatic flourish! Notate your vows as needed. Just underline the words or phrases that you wish to accentuate. Then, practice your vows reciting them with your newly noted emphases.

What should you do next? Use index cards to write a simple outline of your vows for reference. You DO NOT have to write your entire vows on these cards! Outline the key phrases of your vows *in order* and these will help you remember what you have already become familiar with.

Remember, these cards are helpers, a crutch to use so you don't lose your place. When you reference them, do NOT keep your head lowered, *just* reading from them—*instead,* glance at them to find your place like an actor might do from a cue card.

Practice your vows in front of a mirror. Say your vows several times and watch yourself in the mirror to see what you look like as you speak: Are you standing straight or are your shoulders hunched? Are you smiling? This *is* a happy occasion! Do you look sincere? This *is also* a solemn occasion! Just what *does* your body language say about you?

Also, since you have "memorized" all or most of your vows, practice looking straight into your eyes as you would your partner's if he/she was there. After all, when you say your vows, you should be looking at him/her anyway, so why not practice it.

Here's a tip: if you think that you will be using a microphone, practice your speech holding a hairbrush or spoon and speaking into it. Just like you probably did when you were 10 years old and wanted to be a rock star! [See the Appendices for microphone tips].

Practice like this several times *and then* practice in front of your close friend (*you have used him or her an awful lot, so don't forget to give them a "thank you" present, or at least an extra slice of wedding cake*!). Maintain eye contact with him/her as you will your partner on the big day. This may intimidate you at first, but it is an opportunity to conquer your fear in a "real life" situation.

And, as always, allow yourself to be open to any critical feedback about your performance. Now is the time to learn how to make your presentation as perfect as possible!

Even better, have your friend videotape you with a mobile phone to see both your delivery and to see it from the perspective of your partner. Whatever the video shows is what he/she will see at the wedding. (Of course, you could videotape yourself, but having a friend there gives you an audience to practice with and give you feedback.)

Third, learn the territory!

You know that feeling of being a little lost when you start a new job and you don't know where to go or where anything is? The more familiar you are with the site of the ceremony, the more comfortable you'll be on your special day.

Chances are that wherever your wedding will take place is rather unfamiliar to you. It's possible that the time spent at the venue for the wedding rehearsal will be the longest you will be there until the actual ceremony.

Please don't think that you can practice at your wedding rehearsal! At your wedding rehearsal, most officiants just briefly go through the ceremony point by point. They explain what is going on so that you, your partner and the wedding party know *what* is expected and *when* it is expected. They usually don't read the entire service but simply say something like, "I'll say ___ and then you say___." So if you are going to practice your vow presentation in the actual venue, you will have to do it in secret and *before* the wedding rehearsal.

So, if you can, go the actual site of the ceremony and secretly practice your vows. Bring your friend along as a stand-in for your partner. Think of this as the final "dress rehearsal" for your "opening night."

Once you are familiar with the site, you can then practice speaking your vows in your "mind's eye" as you lie in bed each night (or before a nap) and visualize your actually saying your vows. Simply close your eyes, relax, visualize the venue and see yourself saying your vows in your "mind's eye." Hey, if you can lie down, close your eyes and still practice delivering your vows, why not!

ON THE BIG DAY:

The Way is Walked...*You Have Arrived*!

"Their work was done and their undertakings were successful..."

Okay. You've practiced and practiced. The index card(s) are with you, just in case. You have more confidence than you thought you would. So why do you still feel those butterflies?

Well, this is perhaps *THE* biggest moment of your life, so if you weren't at least a *little* nervous, you'd probably be a zombie!

Remember to accept the butterflies. Though everyone attending assumes you'll be a little anxious, no one else *knows* the butterflies are actually there. Own those little buggers!

Chances are you and your partner will be in separate rooms (after all, it *is* considered bad luck for the groom to see the bride before the ceremony) waiting for your "call" to the "stage." Before you walk into wherever the ceremony will actually be performed, take a few moments for yourself and do the following:

+ You are probably not alone, so talk to the person(s) there with you (usually your Best Man or Maid/Matron of Honor, Mums and Dads and assorted groomsmen/bridesmaids). Say something. Verbalize your anxiety: vent, scream, shout, cry—whatever! Get your emotions and anxieties out. These people are there to support you, so use their support. Allow their affirmations to console you. Again, this is like the opening night of a play or the few moments before a boxing bout—use it to psyche yourself up! You know you know what to do and what to say! You *LOVE* him/her dammit!—and you can't wait to get going! You *can* do this! You've got confidence up the wazoo!

+ Do something physical to loosen up! Jog in place! Do a dance! Shake your arms and legs like a scarecrow in a hurricane!

+ Wait for a few minutes after your "exercise" and then take at least 5 deep breaths. Just inhale through your nose and exhale—*slowly*—through your mouth. You will actually feel yourself calm down and your pulse return to somewhat normal.

+ And for heaven's sake, SMILE! Laugh at something too! The sillier the better! It's been medically shown that smiling and laughter both help to lower anxiety and blood pressure levels. So laugh at some silly joke, after all, this *is* a happy occasion!

+ Look at your index cards. Make it a quick glance, though. You know you know your vows, but seeing the cards and actually feeling them reinforces them as a crutch in your mind. You know they are there and you can depend on them should you need them.

+ Your mouth may be dry, so carry a quick dissolve, chewable mint or candy. Why quick dissolve and chewable? You don't want to open your mouth to speak and have a lozenge drop out! Keep a bottle of water with you in the room and take a few sips as well just before you go out.

+ It's also a good idea to keep some facial wipes with you. These pre-moistened towelettes can be used to freshen you face and wipe away any excess sweaty oil. There may not be a restroom nearby, so these replace the cold splash of water you'd probably give yourself to "freshen up." (This tip is mostly for the men since it's pretty safe to assume the ladies will have had their makeup applied by this point.)

Okay, someone has just tapped you on the shoulder or cracked open the door of the room you are in and said, "Okay, it's time!"

THIS IS IT! The curtain's going up!

Suddenly, there you both are, standing in front of everyone, and the officiant has just announced that you have something to say to your partner. You can feel those damn butterflies begin to turn into moths! But . . .

"Hope and fear are phantasms that arise when thinking of the self. When we don't think of our self as self, what do we have to fear?"

In other words, like I said before: Lose your 'self' in the moment. **DON'T PANIC!** Maintain your poise!

Remember what you've learned: you're expected to be a little nervous, so it's okay. No one will even know how nervous you really are unless you exhibit the signs—but you won't! Why? You have confidence in yourself! You've practiced over and over. Besides, this is only a few moments of your entire wedding day!

Turn to your partner. Look at how handsome/beautiful he/she looks! Smile a big, broad smile for both yourself and for him/her.

Take out and hold your index card(s), just in case. (Don't look at them, though; just hold them.)

Look your partner in the eyes, take a deep breath, exhale slowly and say *your* vows.

You will still feel a little nervous, and you know you'll speak a little faster when you have the jitters, so slow down a bit and try to speak normally. Pronounce each word and be certain to enunciate. Speak as conversationally as you can. Keep the inflection in your voice; don't let it become monotone. Make the presentation of our vows as dramatic as you practiced it.

"Admirable words [your vows] can purchase honor;
(its) admirable deeds [your recitation]
can raise their performer above others."

Are your hands shaking just a tad? Got a quiver in your voice? Are your eyes welling up; a tear dropping down your cheek? *GREAT*! Good for you!

It's okay to show emotion, especially now! It proves you're human and that you understand the importance and beauty of this moment in your life. It's nothing to be ashamed of.

Carry on and show your partner how much you care about him/her by saying all the wonderful things you wrote in your vows.

As I said before, "On the day you speak them, you'll feel satisfaction in your heart and see the smile and tears of joy on your partner's face!"

Congratulations!

Vows for a Second Marriage

You are following the Path for the second time but chances are that you have forgotten the way. It has probably been years since you first wrote your wedding vows—if you *did* write them before. (If you didn't, then this chapter is only a brief stopping point, as you are really writing your vows for the first time and need to read this entire book.)

These vows may be similar in form to the vows you stated before—though they obviously need to be specific to your new partner—or they can be completely different; after all, you are older and (I hope) more mature then you were before, so you can write them from that singular perspective. However, whatever you write should always include a personal statement of commitment and love.

Second marriages sometimes mean that there are children, and it is always preferable, with both their consent and understanding, to include them in the ceremony. Such participation is particularly important for younger children. The children's involvement will certainly impress upon them their importance to both you and your new partner.

Your wedding planner can offer some ideas as to just what the children may do to prepare for or partake in the wedding.

One way to do this is to include them in your vows, such as a simple statement of love and respect for them and to welcome them into the family.

You might also consider having them actually participate in the vows ceremony.

With the approval of the officiant, (this is especially necessary for a religious ceremony) you and your partner may wish to recite your vows first and then have the children come forward and respond to the vow questions posed by the officiant, perhaps something like:

Officiant: "Will you accept, love, respect, and abide by your parents?"

Children: "I/We will."

Officiant: "Will you accept, respect, and cherish your new family relationship?"

Children: "I/We will."

And, if applicable:

Officiant: "Will you accept your new siblings, and always show each other love, respect, and understanding?"

Children: "We will."

"I Still Do!" — Vow Renewals

Whether it has been five years, ten years or longer, there is no lovelier way to say "I *still* love you" than to proclaim it anew!

Vow renewals became really popular in the '70's, and since then the renewal or reaffirmation of wedding vows have been a growing trend among couples, especially those married at least five years.

It has become a way to celebrate a special anniversary and to include some of those family and friends from your original wedding, along with new friends and family, especially your children.

Others take it as an opportunity to celebrate after an exceptionally joyous event or to pledge their love anew after a tragic experience. Some do it to seal their reconciliation after a challenging time.

Perhaps you just want to recreate your wedding; maybe as part of a religious service at your house of worship, to show that you still hold your vows sacred.

Or maybe you want to make it the wedding you *wish* you had had originally, whether in a house of worship, banquet hall or your own backyard; or because you eloped.

Whatever *your* reason, one reason these ceremonies are so popular is that vow renewals have no legal requirements, so you may create a ceremony just as you please!

You can make it a simple dinner party for a few family members and friends. Maybe even a beach party, with your vows spoken at sunrise or sunset. How about a picnic at a favorite park? Why not!?

This is *not* a second wedding, so you don't *have* to go overboard following wedding traditions. *New rings? A guest book? Flowers and "bridesmaids"?* Yes or no—whatever *you* want! It can be quiet or boisterous. A simple affair or a large party. Whatever *you* want it to be, <u>it can be</u>!

Note: If you are planning a religious service, check with your officiant as many traditions do not allow you to insert your own vows. You may, however, be allowed to exchange them apart from—before or after—the official service. It never hurts to ask.

. . .

As to what you will say, well, you could repeat your original wedding vows—after all, you *did* keep those old notes and note cards in your "Wedding Memories" box, *didn't you?*

If you did, you are half-way done! All you have to do is frame them with an introduction and a conclusion. Telling everyone how they've held up over the years.

If you didn't keep a copy of your vows (*shame on you!*), then you need to reread this book again or at least look at the outlines and other information provided in the appendices; although that is really no substitute for rereading this book! (Sorry, I know it's more work, but that's what you get for not having a sense of nostalgia!)

However, because vow renewals obviously take place after years of marriage, *these vows* are more like a speech. They incorporate *how* the vow promises have been kept and not just a recitation of the original promises made. Because of this, renewal vows are usually longer than your original vows (see the examples I have given).

. . .

As with your original vows, you'll need to decide:

+ Whether you will write these together or separately, and if separately, you'll have to decide whether to show each other before the renewal ceremony or keep it as a surprise

+ Do you want your renewals to follow the traditional vows or strike out on your own with something original? (You can always include both)

+ Decide how long your vows should be, either by length (a few paragraphs) or by time (a few minutes), however long *you* decide you want them

+ Decide if there are there certain things you wish to include in your vows? Any special words, phrases; any special references; any things the two of you agree *not* to mention!

+ Add a touch of humor?

+ Maybe make a special mention of your children or grandchildren, if appropriate?

You certainly want to express your love and commitment; your continuing friendship and dependence on each other; maybe mention how you've strengthened and supported each other no matter what you've faced and, of course, to sincerely thank each other for being your life partner.

You are welcome to make your renewal as weepy as you please as long as you maintain sincerity and honesty. And JOY! Unlike your wedding when you were starting a life together, you both have "been there, done that" and now is the time to celebrate with a joyous thanksgiving!

For your renewals, you want to express your hopes and promises going forward—much like you did with your original vows—but also take a look back at what both of you have shared and offer sincere thanks for being together and making it as far as you have.

You might say something like this:

"(*Name*) my life has been blessed because of you. You have brought me more joy and love than I know I deserve.

"Life hasn't always been fair or easy, but because of you, your strength, your hope, your love, we made it.

"You are the center of my world and it would crash without you. You truly are all things to me; more than I could ever imagine you would be all those years ago.

"I love you, (*Name*)! I know those three simple words don't seem enough to tell you how much you mean to me and how I feel about you, but if you ask me if I truly love you, I'd quote from our wedding ceremony so long ago and say, 'I do!' or more correctly, 'I *still* do.' *And I always will!*"

Or something more expansive:

"When I look at you, I see the same, young, hopeful face I saw all those years ago. I see the same bright eyes, the same smile; the same look of love. I can't believe it's been ___ years since we said: "I do."

"Every day is like yesterday to me, for it seems as though every day is a new beginning for us, as it seemed when we first married. Every day is filled with promise, with hope, with an ever growing love and respect for each other.

"I know that it hasn't always been easy for us, and I know that a part of that was probably me, and for those parts, I am truly sorry and hope that you can forgive me. Whatever we've faced, though, we've faced together; like we promised, "Through good times and bad." And, *wow!* have there been good times! [here tell a shared, treasured memory, or if appropriate, say 'I look at (*name of child/children*) and realize how blessed we truly are!'] I can only imagine what lies in store for us from this point on; but whatever it is, with you by my side, I know we'll make it.

"Every joy is made the more triumphant because I share it with you; every burden a little less heavy because of you. It is so inadequate to say, "I love you!" but that will have to do. It would take a thesaurus ten thousand pages in length to really find all the words to describe how I feel about you! And I think even *that* would be inadequate!

"So let me just say that you have always been, and remain, my most precious treasure; my one and only true love. I will always be here to guard you, to share with you, to love you . . . forever.

"Like I said, our life has been both rocky and smooth, both joyful and painful, but I can't think of anyone's who hasn't been. I hope for smoothness and joy going forward. But whatever the years have in store for us, the promises I made all those years ago still abide.

"And I hope you don't have to ask, but if you have any doubts, I swear to you and before everyone here, I Love you; and yes, I'd marry you all over again!"

As I have suggested, if you have opened this book to this chapter, you might want to go back and read the entire book; it will certainly help. At least go through the appendices so you have a foundation for writing your vows renewal.

RENEWAL Phrase Cheat Sheet

This short "Cheat Sheet" should get you started with some appropriate phrases. See the "Words and Phrases Cheat Sheet" in the Appendices for additional inspiration.

"I promise anew with a promise not so new . . ."

. . .

"Our love, like our life, is an on-going process, an on-going pleasure . . ."

. . .

"It's a cliché to say that it seems like just yesterday we . . ."

. . .

". . . even stronger than before . . ."

. . .

". . . more strong than ever before . . ."

. . .

"My wish for (your child's name; grandchild's name) is that you are lucky enough to find the love we two both share . . ."

. . .

"If I was uncertain before, now I am sure; for now, I know . . ."

. . .

"Life has changed the both of us, but our love has remained . . ."

. . .

"I pray for good health and long life, if for no other reason than to continue (loving you, my devotion to you, etc.)"

. . .

"Before, now, and forever—YOU are the love of my life!"

. . .

"Love keeps the heart forever young."

. . .

"What I am is what I have become because of you and your love or me."

. . .

"A love like ours comes along once in a lifetime if you're lucky, and your love has made me the luckiest man/woman in the world."

. . .

"I did; I do and I will . . . forever more!"

. . .

"Our lives together have made me older and wiser; well, certainly older . . ."

. . .

"They say "there is no love like a new love" and I know that is so. Because with every sunrise I see you anew, and I love you anew."

. . .

"If, as they say, 'Love is even more lovely, the second time around,' it is lovelier still with the same (man/woman) that second time. And I cannot wait to 'I do' again!"

In Conclusion

Dear Reader:

That's it! If you have trod all the steps along The Way, walked The Path, and followed The Essential Process, then you and your partner will speak the most wonderful vows and create the most wonderful memory of your special day—well, after the memory of the honeymoon that is!

As defined earlier "a vow is a sincere promise, a sacred obligation . . . A vow is a pledge of trust between the couple, and the words spoken should be carefully considered and understood before being pronounced."And I'll bet will be!

It is my sincere hope that you have not only written vows of which you were proud but that by following the process you have learned a little more about yourself and your feelings for your partner.

But your education is far from over—Trust me!

Once you *are* married, every day is another step along The Way of discovery and self-discovery. Each day brings you both closer to one simple goal: "Happily Ever After—Forever!"

Tread The Path carefully; tread together; and take pleasure in every little pebble, pothole—and yes—every rock along The Way. Believe me, you'll learn from every stumble.

And while it may seem that this is the same path that all married couples walk, it is different for each couple. The Way is as unique as the two of you and the Love that you both share. So enjoy your life and every precious moment together. In addition, as you go forward, remember: the journey *is* the destination!

Please allow me once again to offer my heartfelt thanks for trusting me and allowing me to participate in this wonderful event in some small way.

I offer you both this simple toast:

"As you begin your lives together, I wish you both Long Life! Good Health! And Good Luck!"

My Sincere Best Wishes,

J. Thomas Steele

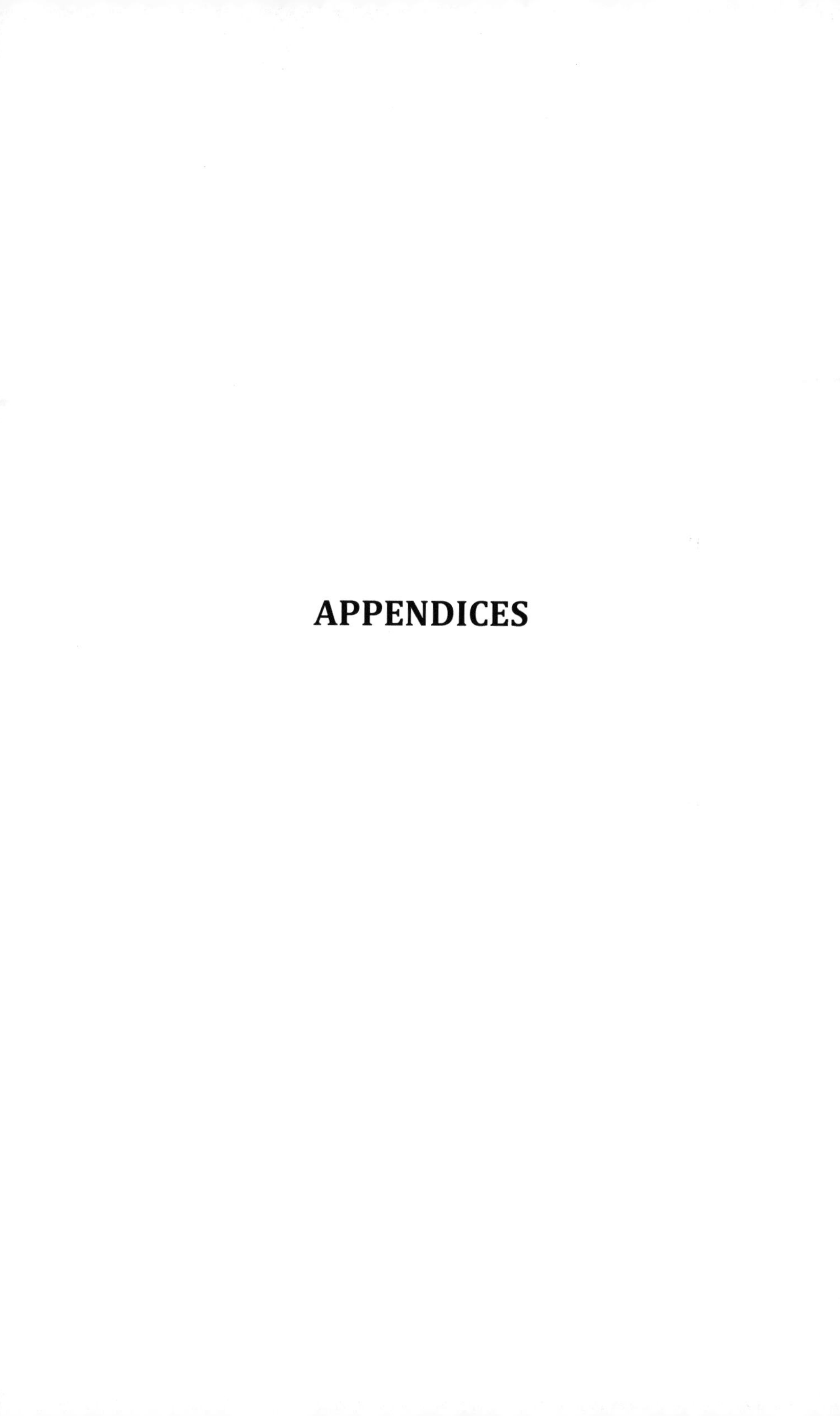

APPENDICES

Please use this page and those at the end of the book for your notes.

Cheat Sheets

Plan of Action Cheat Sheet

Your plan should include agreements with your partner on:

1. An *equal* commitment to the process
2. A time limit for your vows
3. Whether you will write the vows together and each recites the *same* vow
4. Whether to write your *separate* vows together, sharing ideas; or write them *separately*
5. Whether or not you will each share the same beginning of your vows
6. Whether or not to include the same promises in each other's vows; and if so, what should they be?
7. How to keep the vows conversational and not

overly dramatic

8. Your vows general tone--humorous, serious, poetic, romantic, etc.
9. How to respect the individuality of each and allow each of your personalities to show in your vows
10. Allowing some time before you first meet to discuss your vows
11. Agreeing to meet periodically and discuss your progress
12. A deadline to make certain the vows are done on time

Writing Your Vow List Cheat Sheet

Note: Keep ALL papers you create. You can use these for reference for your wedding or anniversary speeches.

~ Sit down in a quiet place and *Brainstorm*! Just let your memories flow!

~ Allow each word or thought to lead to a related word or thought

~ Make either a list or use a topic-mapping technique

~ Write quickly as you think of your partner. Right now neatness doesn't count!

<u>Maybe you might start by</u>:

~ Restating the traditional vows in your own words;

~ Creating a laundry list of the things you love and like about him/her;

~ Jotting down *everything* that's wonderful about him/her!

<u>You might also get a start by answering these questions</u>:

~ How would you describe him/her if someone had never met him/her?

~ What adjectives or simple phrases best identify your beloved?

~ How did you meet?

~ What attracted you to him/her?

~ Think of everything that he/she means to you; how have *you* changed because of his/her influence and love for you?

~ What do you share in common—not just traits, but outlooks, activities, tastes in food, entertainment, life goals, etc.?

~ What are your plans and hopes for your future together?

When done, check your list and look for any comments or descriptions with duplicated words and/or phrases. These must be the most important things you think of your partner.

Remember too that your list can contain quotes from poetry, novels, song lyrics, etc. Use the Appendices for some quick references.

Rewrite these *neatly* on a clean sheet of paper. This is your <u>first edit</u>.

When you are done with this first list, *fuggedaboudit*! Literally. Put it away for several days. You'll come back to it with fresh eyes.

With your fresh eyes, look at your list and organize it.

Group your thoughts into broad categories: 'Love', 'Commitment', etc. You need to take this new list and rewrite what is important into sentences. Don't worry about the rules of English grammar! This is your <u>second edit</u>.

Now show these to a trusted friend and also a married friend for their opinions and insights. After you have incorporated any of their ideas you thought worthy, you need to do a <u>final edit</u>.

Read what you have written and circle the most important things and underline the second most important. Copy these circled lines onto a new sheet of paper and then write the underlined ones.

Next, cut, cut, cut! Until you have a distillation of everything important you need to say. (Remember, you need to meet the agreed upon limit in words or time.)

Finally, look at the two formats and decide which best suits your final draft. Perhaps combine both formats!

Note: These techniques can be applied to other situations where ideas need to be generated and organized, so this book is of benefit beyond writing just your vows!

Topics For Your Vows Cheat Sheet

Aside from the traditional vows ("love, honor, cherish") many modern vows will touch upon these topics, especially in the free form style:

1. Acceptance of each other—the good and not-so-good
2. Communication—discussion between, and listening to, each other
3. Understanding and forgiveness
4. Tolerance of each other and the "little things" that happen
5. The effort it takes to make a marriage work
6. Maintaining good humor and have a willingness to laugh at life's absurdities
7. Learning from each other as you go through life together
8. Beginning and ending each day with a kiss; not going to bed mad
9. Appreciation for each other and all that you share and will share

Words and Phrases Cheat Sheet

Use these as thought starters; choose as appropriate, and use these as keywords in your vows.

Always

Best friend

Blessing

Care for you

Caring

Charity

Cherish (always; our…)

Comfort (in sorrow; you)

Commitment

Companionship

Create together

Declare

Declaration

Depend upon; on whom you may depend

Devotion

Encourage (each other; you); (-ment)

Faith (-ful)

Friend; -ship

From this day (moment) forward (on)

Generous; (-ity)

Generous with your (heart; love)

Honest; (-ty)

Honor

Hope

Humor

Inspiration

Inspire; (-ed)

Inspire me (each other)

Inspired by (you; you're love)

Joy (-ous)

Kindness

Life together

Love

Love you (always; forever)

Marriage

Matrimony

Never again

Never before

Now and forever

Nurture

Open

Partner (-ship)

Pledge

Poetry

Promise

Reassurance

Romance

Through all eternity

To always (be…)

Together (we…)

To grow together … (in mind, body and spirit)

To laugh and cry
To love (forever; no other; only you; you alone)
Triumph

Truthful

Vow

Wed

Wedlock

With no hesitancy (reservation)

With whom to share my life

Worth

Worthy of you

You alone

Miscellaneous Phrases

My heart, my constant heart, contains no doubt…

At last, I know Love's philosophy…

My dear and only love…

You offered such sweet persuasion…

There is no love but you…

There is none but you within my heart…

I listened quietly and my heart told me this was love…

Together forever; forever and true—this is my promise, my pledge to you.

To laugh and cry with you as life presents itself in ease or hardship

You bring elegance to my simple life

I love you as you are; as I hope you love me as I am

Forever; and for you alone…

Delivering Your Vows Cheat Sheet

You *WILL* be nervous! Stay calm and *Don't Worry* about it; worrying about it only makes it worse!

Gain confidence by...

+ Keeping everything in perspective—it's really not a "do or die" kind of thing

+ PRACTICE, PRACTICE, PRACTICE! spending substantial time practicing your vows; it's not "do or die," but it *is* important!

+ Outlining the key phrases of your vows on an index card(s); keep them for a crutch

+ Practicing speaking your vows in front of a mirror to see your body language

+ Then, practicing speaking in front of a close friend

+ Having your friend videotape you to see how you'll look to your partner
+ And if you can, go the actual site of the ceremony so that it becomes more familiar to you. Practice there, if you can.

Once again, The Key is PRACTICE!

On The Day

+ Remember to accept the butterflies! You're expected to be nervous!

+ Talk to the person(s) there with you. Use your friends for comfort and to psyche you up.

+ Do something physical to loosen up: jump, dance, go crazy!

+ After a few minutes rest, take at least 10 deep breaths.

+ Remember to both smile and laugh—they are "good medicine" for anxiety;

+ Look at your index cards. Knowing they are there to fall back on if you need them will give you some confidence.

+ Keep some facial wipes with you to wipe the sweaty oil from your face. (Be careful not to mess up your makeup, ladies!)

+ Carry a quick dissolve mint or candy with you for a dry mouth.

Note: These are valuable tips for *any* speech you may give in the future.

Microphone Cheat Sheet

\+ Most likely the officiant will have already turned the microphone on and preset the volume during a sound check prior to the event.

\+ If holding the microphone, grip it firmly—but not tightly—in the middle of its handle. Judge the firmness of your grip by the weight of the microphone—some are heavier than others. And *please* be careful not to touch or move any buttons on the handle—you might turn the mic off!

\+ Most microphones should be about 4 to 6 inches from your mouth, but *never* more than a hands-width away.

\+ Keep the microphone at a 45-degree angle to your mouth.

\+ Speak into the <u>top surface</u> of the mic. If you hold the mic, DO NOT hold it to the side or close to your chest, as this can cause distortion.

\+ The microphone should have already been tested for feedback, so you shouldn't have to worry about that.

\+ When you do speak, enunciate, pronounce, and speak confidently - after all, you have rehearsed your speech and it should sound great! You will probably be holding your written speech in one hand and the microphone in the other, your hands may shake slightly (that's okay!), just present the speech as you rehearsed it!

+ And how do you rehearse holding the microphone? Hold a hairbrush and practice! Just like you did when you were 10 years old and swore you were on your way to being a rock star!

Religious Wedding Vows

Before you begin to write your vows, you may wish to consider reading these traditional vows from various religious traditions. These are not the entire wedding ceremonies, but the exchange of pledges between The Couple. Therefore, these examples will not include some parts of a particular service.

It may be worth your time to read them *all* to see the different phrases and vows they use, and to note the common elements between them. (Of particular note is how many use the words or a paraphrase from the Book of Common Prayer.) If nothing else, these various vows can be a source of inspiration for writing your own vows.

Note: In my vows research I sometimes came across several vows approved for use in that faith and I have chosen to only show some of these representative examples here. Also, some traditions do not have a formal exchange of vows as we think of them in the West, believing that the *entire* ceremony represents the covenant between The Couple and their God(s). I have chosen to include a few of those traditions here for your reference.

Jewish Vows

In a traditional Jewish ceremony, there is no spoken exchange of vows because the vows are understood to be within the ritual itself. And although the ceremony may differ between the Orthodox, Conservative and Reform branches of Judaism (some Conservative and Reform temples *do* allow couples to exchange both spoken vows and rings) and even among the individual rabbis performing the ceremony, the covenant of marriage is considered sealed when the groom places the ring on the bride's finger.

Before this takes place the traditional Seven Blessings (Sheva B'rachot) is recited:

We praise You, Adonai our God, Ruler of the universe, Creator of the fruit of the vine.

We praise You, Adonai our God, Ruler of the universe, Creator of all things for Your glory.

We praise You, Adonai our God, Ruler of the universe, Creator of man and woman.

We praise You, Adonai our God, Ruler of the universe, who creates us to share with You in life's everlasting renewal.

We praise You, Adonai our God, who causes Zion to rejoice in her children's happy return.

We praise You, Adonai our God, who causes loving companions to rejoice. May these loving companions rejoice as have Your creatures since the days of Creation.

We praise You, Adonai our God, Ruler of the universe, Creator of joy and gladness, friends and lovers, love and kinship, peace and friendship. O God, may there always be heard in the cities of Israel and in the streets of Jerusalem: the sounds of joy and happiness, the voice of loving couples, the shouts of young people celebrating, and the songs of children at play. We praise you, Adonai our God, who causes lovers to rejoice together.

The man then places the ring on his partner's finger and says:

"Behold, you are consecrated to me with this ring, according to the laws of Moses and Israel."

Roman Catholic Vows

The Roman Catholic Church <u>*does not*</u> allow you to use your own wedding vows. Their tradition holds that only the Church provided words offer the essential consent to the marriage. They provide two versions of the vows that The Couple may use:

The traditional vows

"I, (*Name*), take you, (*Name*), to be my (*husband/wife*). I promise to be true to you in good times and in bad, in sickness and in health. I will love you and honor you all the days of my life."

In the dioceses of the United States, the following form may also be used.

"I, (*Name*), take you, (*Name*), for my lawfully wedded (*husband/wife*), to have and to hold, from this day forward, for better, for worse, for richer, for poorer, in sickness and in health, until death do us part."

Book of Common Prayer Marriage Service

This is NOT the revised, more modern language, service from 2000. Though this newer one is now often used in Anglican and Episcopal ceremonies, I've listed the older, more traditional service here.

"_(Name)_, wilt thou have this (*man/woman*) to be thy wedded (*husband/wife*), to live together after God's ordinance in the holy estate of Matrimony? Wilt thou love (*him/her*), comfort (*him/her*), honor and keep (*him/her*), in sickness and in health: and, forsaking all other, keep thee only unto (*him/her*) so long as ye both shall live?"

The (*man/woman*) answers: I will.

And, after taking the partner's hand repeats:

"I (*Name*) take thee (*Name*) to be my wedded (*husband/wife*), to have and to hold, from this day forward, for better, for worse, for richer, for poorer, in sickness and in health, to love and to cherish, till death us do part, according to God's holy ordinance: And thereto I plight thee my faith (troth)."

Baptist Vows

"I (*Name*) take you (*Name*) to be my wedded (*husband/wife*), and promise to build together a Christian home under the Lordship of Jesus Christ. I will provide for you and protect you, cherish and grant you honor, as a fellow heir of the grace of God.

I will be faithful to you, and honest with you, I will stand with you in sickness or in health, in good times or hard till death alone shall part us"

Lutheran Vows

Evangelical Lutheran Church in America

"In the presence of God and this community, I, (*Name*), take you, (*Name*), to be my (*husband/wife*); to have and to hold from this day forward, in joy and in sorrow, in plenty and in want, in sickness and in health, to love and to cherish, as long as we both shall live. This is my solemn vow."

Others also say:

"I take you, (*Name*), to be my (*husband/wife*), and these

things I promise you: I will respect, trust, help, and care for you; I will forgive you as we have been forgiven; and I will share my life with you, through the best and worst of all that is to come, until death parts us."

Lutheran Church Missouri Synod

"I, (*Name*), in the presence of God and these witnesses, take you, (*Name*), to be my (*husband/wife*), to have and to hold from this day forward, for better, for worse, for richer, for poorer, in sickness and in health, to love and to cherish, until death parts us, and I pledge you my faithfulness."

Also,

"I take you, (*Name*), to be my (*husband/wife*) from this day forward, to join with you and share all that is to come, and I promise to be faithful to you until death parts us."

Methodist

"__*(Name)*__, will you have __*(Name)*__ to be your (*husband/wife*), to live together in holy marriage? Will you love (*him/her*), comfort (*him/her*), honor, and keep (*him/her*) in sickness and in health, and forsaking all others, be faithful to (*him/her*) as long as you both shall live?"

"In the Name of God, I, (*Name*), take you, (*Name*), to be my (*husband/wife*) to have and to hold, from this day forward, for better, for worse, for richer, for poorer, in sickness and in health, to love and to cherish, until we are parted by death. This is my solemn vow."

Presbyterian

" __*(Name)*__, wilt thou have this (*man/woman*) to be thy (*husband/wife*), and wilt thou pledge thy faith to (*him/her*), in all love and honor, in all duty and service, in all faith and tenderness, to live with (*him/her*), and cherish (*him/her*), according to the ordinance of God, in the holy bond of marriage?"

"I, (*Name*), take you (*Name*) to be my (*husband/wife*), and I do promise and covenant, before God and these witnesses, to be your loving and faithful (*husband/wife*), in plenty and in want, in joy and in sorrow, in sickness and in health, as long as we both shall live."

Unitarian/Universalist

True to its teachings, The Unitarian Universalist Church leaves both the structure of the wedding ceremony and the actual words used in the ceremony to the discretion of the individual minister. However, the words are usually a paraphrase of traditional Christian wedding vows. These are two representative vows.

"I, (*Name*), take you, (*Name*), to be my (*husband/wife*), to have and to hold, from this day forward, for better, for worse, for richer, for poorer, in sickness and in health, to love and cherish always."

Some also choose:

"I, (*Name*), choose you,(*Name*), to be the (*husband/wife*) of my days, to be the (*mother/father*) of my children, to be the companion of my house; I shall keep with you what share of trouble and sorrow our lives may lay upon us, and I shall share with you, our store of goodness and plenty and love."

United Church of Christ

"(*Name*), I give myself to you in the covenant of marriage. I promise to love and sustain you in this covenant, from this day forward, in sickness and in health, in plenty and in want, in joy and in sorrow, as long as we both shall live."

Also,

"I, (*Name*), take you, (*Name*), to be my (*husband/wife*), and I promise to love and sustain you in the bonds of marriage from this day forward, in sickness and in health, in plenty and in want, in joy and in sorrow, till death shall part us, according to God's holy ordinance."

Other Religious Wedding Vows

Quaker Vows

A Society of Friends wedding ceremony is very much a congregational affair, the focus of which is on silent mutual prayer. During the prayer, both the bride and groom agree to commit to one another, remain loyal, and to always love each other. Following the silent prayer, the couple stands up, holds hands, and recites vows similar to this: "In the presence of God and these our friends, I take thee to be my (*husband/wife*), promising with Divine assistance to be unto thee a loving and faithful (*husband/wife*) so long as we both shall live."

Eastern Orthodox Vows

Like the Quakers, many branches of the Orthodox Church use silent vows during the wedding ceremony. This quiet, introspective prayer is one in which the couple promises to be loyal and loving to each other.

However, in the Russian Orthodox tradition the vows are spoken aloud:

"I, <u>Name</u>, take you, <u>Name</u>, as my wedded (*husband/wife*) and I promise you love, honor and respect; to be faithful to you, and not to forsake you until death do us part. So help me God, one in the Holy Trinity and all the Saints."

Buddhist Vows

Although Buddhist weddings are traditionally regarded as secular affairs in Buddhist countries, The Couple usually seeks a blessing from the monks at their local temple after completion of the civil ceremony. Buddhist belief allows each couple to decide what issues are most important in their marriage as long as each pledge to seek and acknowledge a greater Truth than themselves and this existence. Therefore, each couple can create their own unique set of marriage vows. As such, there are no standard wedding vows to recite, although most vows include the promises of love, companionship, friendship, mutual respect and admiration, commitment to each other through good and bad times, fidelity, etc.

Hindu Vows

There are many customary rituals within a traditional Hindu ceremony. As with Buddhism, there are no "vows" in the Western sense. However, the Seven Steps, or *Saptha Padhi,* in which the couple circuits the Holy Flame (honoring the fire god, Agni, who blesses their union) seven times, spell out the promises they make to each other and without which no Hindu marriage is considered complete and binding. As The Couple begins their walk around the sacred flame, the groom leads during the first three circuits and the bride leads the remaining four.

The vows follow as such:

First Vow: A prayer for the blessing of nourishing food, and respect for the household and living together

Second Vow: A prayer for physical, mental and spiritual strength; and for a peaceful and healthy life together.

Third Vow: A prayer for both prosperity and wisdom; and to affirm a mutual commitment to each other through times of both joy and sorrow

Fourth Vow: A prayer for mutual happiness in the marriage through love and trust

Fifth Vow: A prayer for happy, healthy children and for the happiness of all beings

Sixth Vow: A prayer for harmony and for a long, happy life together.

Seventh Vow: A prayer for a true lifelong companionship, partnership, and friendship.

Muslim Vows

The traditional Muslim ceremony (*nikah*) concerns both the uniting of husband and wife and the union of souls, and focuses on the moment when the *imam* (cleric) explains the meaning of marriage and the nature of the bride and groom's commitment and responsibilities to each other and to Allah. After which, the couple acknowledges their consent to be husband and wife. While there is no usual exchange of vows, some couples recite the following:

Bride: "I, *(Name)* , offer you myself in marriage in accordance with the instructions of the Holy Qur'an and the Holy Prophet, peace and blessing be upon Him. I pledge, in honesty and with sincerity, to be for you an obedient and faithful wife."

Groom: "I pledge, in honesty and sincerity, to be for you a faithful and helpful husband."

Sample Wedding Vows

Note: Many secular vows can become religious vows by the *inclusion* of the name of a deity. "With God's guidance . . ." "Through the Lord . . ." "May the Most Holy grant . . ." "Almighty God . . ." and so on. Conversely, a religious vow can become non-religious by *removing* a reference to a deity.

. . .

"I promise to be true to you through the good times and the bad, through illness and in health. I will love, cherish and honor you all the days of my life."

. . .

"I will cherish our love, now and forever. I will be faithful to you alone. I will honor our friendship. I will honor the trust we share. I will cherish our time together, through the best or the worst of times. I give you my vow to honor and cherish *you*, above all."

. . .

"Knowing that you alone are my faithful and constant companion in life, my one, and only true love, I vow before all, in the presence of God, to be *your* faithful and constant companion through joy and sorrow, sickness and health, cherishing every day that we are together for as long as we both shall live."

. . .

"I honor you and vow to always do so. I cherish you and vow to do so always. I cherish our friendship and vow to do so always. I shall be your companion and champion through all our days together. Through good and bad times and through illness and health; and I shall love you, and only you, through all the days of our lives."

. . .

"Time, for me, began when I met you. From that first second, I loved you. And I shall until my last. Every moment we are together, Time seems to fade, to stand still. YOU fill my every second; and still, Time passes too swiftly. Before I know it the seconds have turned to minutes, to hours, to days. I am lost in Time . . . I am lost in YOU!

"Time began with you and though Time will always pass, as it must, every moment of my life is filled with you; every tick of the clock is an eternity of love shared with you. And as the hands of the clock ever turn in a circle, its movement is like the wedding ring I (will) wear symbolizing my love for you—endless . . . forever . . . across *ALL* Time!"

. . .

"I love you. I have faith in my love, and in *you* . . . and in *us*. I see hope in my love, and in *you* . . . and in *us*. Now many define 'faith' as confidence, and 'hope' as trust—accepting without evidence.' I believe in love. For to me, the evidence is there. It is in *my* heart and in everything *you* do. I see it in your walk, in your smile. I hear it in your voice, in your every word. I feel it in your touch. My every sense of you shows the evidence.

"My belief, my faith, my love is true, now and forever. I recognize it, and *you,* as a gift. It is something without price, something I will always cherish. It abides with me forever. At this blessed moment, and forever more, I agree with Saint Paul when he wrote, "But now abides faith, hope, love . . . these three; and the greatest of these is love." That is the gift you have given me and the gift I share with you."

. . .

"It sounds so silly to say something like, 'There was no me before you,' for I was here long before I met you. But the *me* that was *then* is certainly not the *me* that stands before you today. The better part of the old me remains, but only because you sanctified those better parts with your love. The rest of me is new because of your love.

"You have shaken me up, and shaken me out . . . and I have grown because of you and your love. The rusty iron that once guarded my heart and soul for those many years has been changed to shiny gold by *your* love: changed from base to precious; from hard to malleable. My prayer for our future is that I may always find the better part of me through your love and that I may, in some small way, be worthy enough to have you always accept the love I bear; and to share the beauty that I find in you."

. . .

"There was a time I could never imagine myself getting married! There was a time I could only see myself alone,
a future filled with uncertainty. There was a time I could never imagine myself with someone as beautiful, as caring, as loving, as wonderful as you. There was a time I could not

imagine you in my life, and now I cannot imagine my life without you!"

. . .

"Because I love you, with all my heart and soul, I find my life forever changed. Because of you, I know there are such things as hope and love, and I find a faith in myself and in my future that I had never known before. Because of you, I find more joy in my life than I have ever known and more love in my heart than I could ever imagine it could hold. Because I find that there is no one in my life that I love the way that I love you, I pledge myself yours forever. And should you, as our years together pass by, ever doubt my love—just ask me why I love you and I will answer, "Just because."

. . .

"Today our lives begin anew. Our past is history. From this moment on there is only the ever-present 'now'. And so I vow to you and all assembled to love you now; to cherish you now; to be true unto you now. As we grow together and face whatever becomes our 'now' I will be your constant companion. I will be with you. Simply put: I love you!—Now . . . and forever!"

. . .

"While the definition of Love will change over time as we live our lives together, I promise that Love itself will always be there. A Love as rich, vibrant and all-encompassing in the future, as it is now. And I swear that whatever we face in the years to come, we shall do so together, in faith and in Love."

. . .

Many vows conclude with simple statements, such as:

"You and I, in Love . . . forever."

Or, "I do; I will, and I always shall!"

Quotations

These are a few short quotations appropriate for wedding vows. You can use the entire quote, phrases from it or a paraphrase as you see fit.

You may even have your own favorite quotations, poems or song lyrics you may wish to quote.

Remember, though, that your vows are usually brief, so choose wisely!

Note: Errors in spelling and grammar are in the original.

. . .

Thomas a Kempis (1380-1471) German Christian writer

"Love feels no burden, thinks nothing of trouble, attempts what is above its strength, pleads no excuse of impossibility; for it thinks all things lawful for itself, and all things possible." *The Imitation of Christ (1418)* Book III chapter 5 - "The Wonderful Effect of Divine Love"

"Nothing is sweeter than love, nothing more courageous, nothing higher, nothing wider, nothing more pleasant, nothing fuller, and nothing better in heaven or on earth . . ."

"Love is active, sincere, affectionate, pleasant and amiable; courageous, patient, faithful, prudent, long-suffering, resolute, and never self-seeking."

. . .

Aristotle (384 BCE-322 BCE) Greek philosopher

"Love is composed of a single soul inhabiting two bodies." Assertion attributed to Aristotle in *Lives of Eminent Philosophers* by Diogenes Laërtius

. . .

Saint Augustine (354-430) early Christian theologian

"As love grows within you, so too does beauty grow; for love is the beauty in your soul." *Homilies on the First Epistle of John*, Ninth Homily

. . .

Honore de Balzac (1799-1850) French novelist

"One should believe in marriage as in the immortality of

the soul." *Comedie Humaine* (1841)

"True love is eternal, infinite and always like itself. It's always equal and pure. Without violent demonstrations: It is seen with white hairs and is always young at heart." *Ibid.*

. . .

The Bible King James Version

1 John 3:18 ". . . let us not love in word, neither in tongue; but in deed and in truth."

. . .

Emily Brontë (1818-1848) English author

"He's more myself than I am. Whatever our souls are made of, his and mine are the same." *Wuthering Heights* (1847) Ch. 9

(Change to "She's" and "hers" as appropriate.)

. . .

Elizabeth Barret Browning (1806-1861) English poet

"If thou must love me, let it be for naught

Except for love's sake only. Do not say

"I love her for her smile—her look—her way

Of speaking gently,—for a trick of thought

That falls in well with mine, and certes brought
A sense of pleasant ease on such a day"—
For these things in themselves, Beloved, may
Be changed, or change for thee,—and love, so wrought,
May be unwrought so. Neither love me for
Thine own dear pity's wiping my cheeks dry,—
A creature might forget to weep, who bore
Thy comfort long, and lose thy love thereby!
But love me for love's sake, that evermore
Thou may'st love on, through love's eternity."

Sonnets from the Portuguese, No. XIV

"How do I love thee? Let me count the ways.
I love thee to the depth and breadth and height
My soul can reach, when feeling out of sight
For the ends of Being and ideal Grace.
I love thee to the level of everyday's
Most quiet need, by sun and candlelight.
I love thee freely, as men strive for Right;
I love thee purely, as they turn from Praise.
I love thee with the passion put to use
In my old griefs, and with my childhood's faith.
I love thee with a love I seemed to lose

With my lost saints,—I love thee with the breath,

Smiles, tears, of all my life!—and, if God choose,

I shall but love thee better after death."

Sonnets from the Portuguese, No. XLIII

. . .

Robert Browning (1812-1889) English poet

"Grow old with me! The best is yet to be."

Rabbi Ben Ezra Line1, *Dramatis Personae* (1864)

. . .

Robert Burns 1759-1796 Scottish poet

"To see her is to love her, And love but her forever;

For nature made her what she is,

And never made anither! (another)"

Bonny Lesley (1792)

. . .

Emily Dickinson (1830-86) American poet

"That love is all there is / Is all we know of love."

Poem #1765

. . .

George Eliot (Mary Ann Evans) (1819-1880) English novelist

"What greater thing is there for two human souls, than to feel that they are joined for life--to strengthen each other in all labor, to rest on each other in all sorrow, to minister to each other in all pain, to be one with each other in silent unspeakable memories at the moment of the last parting?" *Adam Bede* (1859)

. . .

Ralph Waldo Emerson (1803-1882) American essayist/poet

"What lies behind us, and what lies before us are tiny matters compared to what lies within us." *Attributed*

. . .

Desiderius Erasmus (1466-1536) Dutch philosopher

"For anyone who loves intensely lives not in himself but in the object of his love, and the further he can move out of himself into his love, the happier he is." *Praise of Folly* (1511)

St. Francis of Assisi (Giovanni di Pietro di Bernardone) (1181/82-1226) Roman Catholic friar

"Lord, make me an instrument of your peace. Where this is hatred, let me sow love; Where there is injury, pardon; Where there is doubt, faith; Where there is despair, hope; Where there is darkness, light And where there is sadness, joy.

"O Divine Master, grant that I may not so much seek to be consoled as to console; to be understood as to understand; to be loved as to love. For it is in giving that we receive; It is in pardoning that we are pardoned, and it is in dying that we are born to eternal life."

. . .

Johann Wolfgang von Goethe (1749-1832) German poet/dramatist

"Love does not dominate; it cultivates." *Das Märchen* (1795)

. . .

Victor Hugo (1802-1885) French novelist/poet

"Life's greatest happiness is to be convinced we are loved, loved for ourselves, or rather loved in spite of ourselves." *Les Miserables (1862)*

. . .

John Keats (1795-1821) English poet

"I love you more in that I believe you had liked me for my own sake and for nothing else." *Letter to Fanny Brawne, July 8, 1819*

"My Creed is Love and you are its only tenant." *Letter to Fanny Brawne,* 13 Oct 1819

"A thing of beauty is a joy forever:
Its loveliness increases; it will never
Pass into nothingness . . ."

Endymion (1818)

. . .

Julian of Norwich (1342-1413) English Medieval mystic

"Our life is all grounded and rooted in love, and without love we may not live." *Revelations of Divine Love* (c. 1393), Ch. 48

. . .

Helen Keller (1880-1968) American author/activist

"The best and most beautiful things in the world cannot be seen or even touched. They must be felt with the heart." *The Story of My Life* (1905)

. . .

Baron Eligius Franz Joseph von Münch-Bellinghausen (1806-1871) Austrian playwright, poet

"Two souls with but a single thought,

Two hearts that beat as one."

Der Sohn der Wildnis (1842) Act II

(*Often misattributed to John Keats*)

. . .

Lao Tzu (ca. 6th Century BCE) Legendary Chinese philosopher

"Being deeply loved by someone gives you strength, while loving someone deeply gives you courage." *Tao Te Ching*

"Love is of all passions the strongest, for it attacks simultaneously the head, the heart, and the senses." *Ibid.*

"Kindness in words creates confidence. Kindness in thinking creates profoundness. Kindness in giving creates love." *Ibid.*

"Simplicity, patience, compassion. These three are your greatest treasures. Simple in actions and thoughts, you return to the source of being. Patient with both friends and enemies, you accord with the way things are. Compassionate toward yourself, you reconcile all beings in the world." *Ibid.*

"Marriage is three parts love and seven parts forgiveness . . ." *Ibid.*

"Explore within and discover what lies within you. For when we find ourselves, we are more easily found by others. Without words or understanding how, lovers find each other. The moment of finding is unsought and always a surprise, akin to meeting an old friend, just one never before known.

Life and marriage are a wondrous journey; they are an ever-unfolding chance to rediscover both ourselves and our beloved again and again on this shared path.

The only constant thing is change. Embrace it and let it lead you to many a glorious tomorrow." *Ibid.*

[Other quotes appear in the text]

. . .

Blaise Pascal (1623-1662) French philosopher

"The heart has its reasons, which Reason does not know." *Pensées* (1670) Section IV "On the Means of the Belief"

"When one does not love too much, one does not love enough." *Ibid.*

. . .

Plato Greek philosopher (424/428 BCE-348/47 BCE)

"Every heart sings a song, incomplete, until another heart whispers back. Those who wish to sing always find a song. At the touch of a lover, everyone becomes a poet."

The Symposium (385-370 BCE)

. . .

Edgar Allan Poe American author (1809-1849)

"We loved with a love that was more than love."

Annabel Lee (1849)

. . .

Quran (Koran) ayah (verses)

[25:74] "And they say, "Our Lord, let our spouses and children be a source of joy for us, and keep us in the forefront of the righteous."

[30:21] "Among His proofs is that He created for you spouses from among yourselves, in order to have tranquility and contentment with each other, and He placed in your hearts love and care towards your spouses."

. . .

Jalal-Uddin Rumi (1207-1273) Persian poet/mystic

"Love will find its way through all languages on its own."

"Love rests on no foundation. It is an endless ocean, with no beginning or end."

"We love: that's why life is full of so many wonderful gifts."

. . .

George Sand (Amantine-Lucile-Aurore Dupin) (1804—1876) French novelist

"There is only one happiness in life, to love and be loved."

Letter, dated 1862

. . .

William Shakespeare (1564-1616) English poet and playwright

"No sooner met but they looked; no sooner looked but they loved; no sooner loved but they sighed; no sooner sighed but they asked one another the reason; no sooner knew the reason but they sought the remedy; and in these degrees have they made a pair of stairs to marriage . . ."

As You Like It Act V sc. 2 (1596-1600)

"Doubt thou the stars are fire; Doubt that the sun doth move; Doubt truth to be a liar; But never doubt I love." *Hamlet* (1603) Act II scene ii

"God, the best maker of all marriages, Combine [our] hearts in one." *Henry V* Act I sc. 2

"I do not wish any companion in the world but you."

The Tempest Act III scene I (1610-11)

"There is so much more that I could say, but as Shakespeare said, 'Men of few words are the best men.'"

Henry V Act III sc. 2 (1598-99)

"If I could write the beauty of your eyes, And in fresh numbers number all your graces, The age to come would say, this poet lies, Such heavenly touches ne'er touch'd earthly faces." Sonnet 17

. . .

Franz Schubert (1797-1828) Austrian composer

"Happy is the man who finds a true friend, and far happier is he who finds that true friend in his wife."

. . .

Sophocles Greek playwright (496 BCE-406 BCE)

"One word frees us of all the weight and pain of life: That word is love." *Oedipus at Colonus* (ca. 401BCE) line 1616-18

. . .

Alfred, Lord Tennyson (1809-1892) British poet

"If I had a flower for every time I thought of you, I could walk in my garden forever." *Locksley Hall* (1835, pub. 1842)

Henry David Thoreau (1817-1862) American poet/ essayist

"Love must be as much a light, as it is a flame."

. . .

Leo Tolstoy (1828-1910) Russian writer/philosopher

"He felt now that he was not simply close to her, but that he did not know where he ended and she began."

Anna Karenina (1875-1877; 1878) Ch. 14

"All, everything that I understand, I understand only because I love." *War and Peace* 1865-69

"It is not beauty that endears, it's love that makes us see beauty." *Ibid.*

. . .

Mark Twain (1835-1910) American author/humorist

". . . to get the full value of joy, you must have someone to divide it with." epigram from *Pudd'nhead Wilson's Calendar* in *Following the Equator* (1897)

. . .

Virgil (Publius Vergilius Maro) (70 BCE-19 BCE) Roman poet

"Love conquers all things; let us too give into love." Book X, line 69 (translated by John Dryden).

"Now I know what love is." *Eclogues* Book VIII, line 43.

. . .

John Wesley (1703-1791) English clergyman/reformer

"An ounce of love is worth a pound of knowledge."

Letter to Joseph Benson (7 November 1768)

. . .

Walt Whitman (1819-1892) American poet

"The strongest and sweetest songs yet remain to be sung." *Leaves of Grass* (1855/1892)

About the Author

For over forty years, J. Thomas Steele has helped countless brides, grooms, and members of the wedding party write both vows and wedding speeches. His son's engagement encouraged him to "help others help themselves" by writing this book and the others in *The Wedding Series.*

Mr. Steele has an eclectic range of interests, from history and philosophy to food and children's stories, and hopes to share this enthusiasm for both learning and a good tale with his readers. He lives in South Florida and writes both fiction and non-fiction.

Other books in ***The Wedding Series***:

On premarital preparation: *Questions for Couples: What to Ask Before You Say "I Do": A Primer for Planning Your Future Together and A Guide to What to Expect From Premarital Counseling*

On writing and delivering, The Couple's wedding speech: *YOUR Wedding Speech Made Easy: The "How-to" Guide for The Couple (Writing and Delivering YOUR Perfect Wedding Speech)*

On writing and delivering speeches for members of the wedding party: *YOUR Wedding Speech Made Easy: The "How-to" Guide for the Father of the Bride, the Best Man . . . and Everyone Else! (Writing and Delivering YOUR Perfect Wedding Speech)*

For more information about J. Thomas Steele, please visit his author page on Amazon's Author Central page at: amazon.com/author/jthomassteele

Like him on Facebook at:
www.facebook.com/jthomassteele.author

NOTES

NOTES

Printed in Poland
by Amazon Fulfillment
Poland Sp. z o.o., Wrocław